NATIVE AMERICAN
BEADWORK

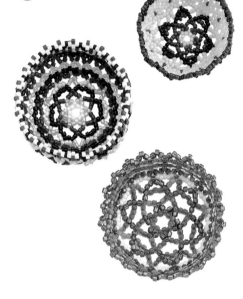

NATIVE AMERICAN BEADWORK

Projects & Techniques from the Southwest

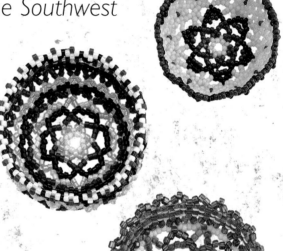

Theresa Flores Geary

Sterling Publishing Co., Inc.
New York

Edited by Jeanette Green
Designed by Judy Morgan
Photographs by Nancy Palubniak
Step photos, scans, and drawings by Theresa Flores Geary
Technical design support by Eileen Laibinis

Library of Congress Cataloging-in-Publication Data
Geary, Theresa Flores.
    Native American beadwork : projects & techniques from the Southwest /
Theresa Flores Geary.
      p. cm.
    Includes index.
    ISBN 1-4027-0330-9
   1. Beadwork—Patterns. 2. Indian beadwork—Southwestern States—Handbooks,
manuals, etc. I. Title.
TT860.G43 2003
745.58′2′08997-dc21   2003005732

10 9 8 7 6 5 4 3 2 1

Published by Sterling Publishing Co., Inc.
387 Park Avenue South, New York, NY 10016
©2003 by Theresa Flores Geary
Distributed in Canada by Sterling Publishing
℅ Canadian Manda Group, One Atlantic Avenue, Suite 105
Toronto, Ontario, Canada M6K 3E7
Distributed in Great Britain by Chrysalis Books
64 Brewery Road, London N7 9NT, England
Distributed in Australia by Capricorn Link (Australia) Pty. Ltd.
P.O. Box 704, Windsor, NSW 2756, Australia

Sterling ISBN 1-4027-0330-9

For my mother, Anna Flores,
and for the grandmothers of the
San Carlos Apache tribe

CONTENTS

NATIVE AMERICAN BEADWORK FROM THE SOUTHWEST

Beadwork has an amazing history through the millennia. Even with so many brilliant examples of beadwork found on all continents except Antarctica, the Native American style of beading remains extremely popular worldwide. It is characterized by bright colors, bold designs, and extravagant beauty with natural themes. Embedded in the designs are symbols of spiritual significance to the native cultures originating them.

Initially known for the use of natural materials and organic beads, contemporary Native American beaders today are taking full advantage of modern technology to acquire the most exotic beads and components for their art medium. Beads made of glass, gemstones, and precious metals are used in addition to beads made of wood, seeds, nuts, shells, bone, horn, animal teeth, vertebrae, and porcupine quills.

Traditional Native American beadwork from the Southwest is often defined by the specific opaque colors often seen in museum pieces. What some historians ignore is that, centuries ago, native beaders had more limited access to various bead sizes and colors. Thanks to modern globalization and relatively easy transportation, a wide variety of beading materials can be imported from all parts of the world and sold in local markets at reasonable prices.

Many contemporary beaders appreciate the wealth of available resources that allow them to maximize their creative expression. For example, heishe was traditionally made from gemstones or shells that are individually hand-drilled and then strung. The resulting strand was rolled on hard rock to form a smooth strand of beads. The process is similar to rolling clay, except gemstones and shells are hard. Rolling the heishe beads until smooth is very labor-intensive and time-consuming. Similarly, seeds or nuts used for beads must be individually harvested and hand drilled before stringing. Other natural materials, like bear claws and porcupine quills, are dangerous to collect.

With bead technology flourishing, modern beaders invest less time in securing their materials and more time in the creative process. Modern technology uses equipment to polish stones and drill beads. Laser equipment can precision cut glass beads from cylinders. In earlier centuries, artwork was more of a luxury, and most beadwork seen in museums today had originally served as functional or ceremonial art. Very few museum pieces can be classified as merely personal adornment, like jewelry commonly worn today.

Aspects of functional and ceremonial art are still evident in Native American beading. Many old native traditions, values, and spiritual beliefs are enjoying a resurgence of attention through the medium of beadwork. Use of native symbolism, designs, and colors reveal the underlying spiritual foundation many native beaders still hold dear. Keeping in mind that there are numerous Native American tribes with different genetic, cultural, linguistic, and historical backgrounds, the specific symbolism found in native beadwork can vary from one artist to another or from one tribe to another. In addition, ceremonial beadwork is unlike that made strictly for the tourist trade. Generally, the first line of authority in the interpretation of any art is the artist.

The projects in this book include beading techniques currently taught to interested students, both native and non-native. Native American beaders from the Southwest, perhaps more than those from any other region, have had a strong influence on beaders. This is evident by the fact that common names used for stitches and techniques, such as the Comanche or Apache weave, often relate to specific functions or names of Southwest tribes. The Apache weave is often seen in earrings made for tourists by Apaches. This weave is also called Comanche weave, another tribe's name. Of course, Navajos, as well as other peoples from around the world, also create the same type of earring, but it has been most popularly associated with these two tribes, the Apaches and Comanches. Some beading books credit the Egyptian era for this type of stitch, also called brick stitch. Navajos are world-renowned for their woven rugs, and some incorporate similar awesome designs in their beadwork patterns. While some designs have a commonly visible theme or representation, such as mountains, clouds, or animals, this does not preclude the possibility of a different symbolic meaning intended by the artist.

Modern laws deny anyone from holding a copyright on a technique or a design found in nature. Geometric shapes, like concentric diamonds, are often seen in loomed beadwork because the stitch lends itself to geometric designs. Who originated a stitch or technique does not matter as much as what is done with that technique. Today, as in the past, beaders' use of a frequently seen design or pattern may be strictly dictated by its popular consumer appeal.

Peyote stitch was named after a ceremonial rattle or fan that was beaded with a particular stitch that could accommodate a three-dimensional object. Literature on beadwork techniques usually credits Native Americans with this technique since its origins were first documented on the continent of North America. Naturally,

many beaders who want to learn peyote stitch have no idea of its history or of native functions but still appreciate the peyote stitch's usefulness for beading around a three-dimensional object.

Not so ironically, American Indians use the peyote gourd for making not just the rattle and fan but also for carrying the peyote cactus that's used ceremonially. The native word *pejuta* is roughly translated to mean "medicine."

Semantics aside, the significance of beadwork and beads is fascinating to explore. Paraphrasing Black Elk, a renowned holy man of the Lakota Sioux, "the power of an object is in the symbolism." With that in mind, each project in these chapters highlights designs and symbols that can provide insight into the subtle meaning and beauty of the beaded objects. The symbolism of these projects, described in the opening paragraphs of each chapter, is not intended to be all-inclusive or authoritative; we cannot speak for any particular tribe or artist.

Beading can also be therapeutic—its repetition and creativity healing to body, mind, and spirit. (The spiritual realm may be more difficult to explore.) Bead therapy is a relatively new concept in the health field; it can be used with many different clinical populations dealing with physical, emotional, mental, or spiritual problems. In many Native American communities, bead therapy is more commonly accepted because of its historical association with spiritual ceremonies. However, not all Southwest tribes are known for their appreciation of beadwork. Some in North and South America excel in virtually lost arts like basket weaving, quillwork, stone carving, sand painting, pottery, rug weaving, silversmithing, leatherwork, masks, musical instruments, and quilt making.

Several quaint tales describe how native populations in the New World received glass beads. Beads made of natural materials, like seashells, stones, seeds, animal horn, antlers, and bones have been found on all continents. However, in ancient times, those types of handmade beads usually involved a great deal of work and were somewhat irregular. Modern glass beads are smooth, shiny, colorful, and consistently shaped.

One story relates a native woman's reaction when she first saw and felt the small glass beads. She called them "little spirit seeds," a gift of the Great Spirit. To this day, these beads are still called seed beads. Many beaders appreciate the notion that when we create beaded objects, we are sowing seeds of a positive nature as an expression of our gratitude for the gift of beads.

Although archaeologists have documented the existence of beads since ancient times, the modern word *bead* comes from the Anglo-Saxon term *biddan,* which means "to pray" or "to meditate." Around the world, cultures and religions, like Catholicism, Buddhism, and Hinduism, have a long history of using some type of prayer beads, presumably to support their religious or spiritual beliefs. While it's difficult to define a general, much less a universal concept of prayer or spirituality, its many expressions have found that beads, whether used for counting, remembering, ritual, or repetition, appear to give body to the soul's desires.

Beads and their symbolism are an integral part of numerous healing ceremonies and ceremonial objects. Most beadwork seen in museums can be identified as ceremonial if one understands

the symbolism written into the beadwork with colors and designs. These physical artifacts only hint at their uses, which can excite extensive speculations of archaeologists and museum staffs. Many modern native healers and traditionalists have carried on the knowledge of our ancestors and continue to pass it on to new generations through oral tradition and art.

Making a medicine bag is another therapeutic use of beadwork. Here we use the term *medicine* in an all-encompassing way; it means anything that can improve the physical, mental, emotional, or spiritual health of the maker. (Find more details about Native American spiritual symbolism and philosophy in Chapters 6, 8, and 13.)

You'll be able to apply the beading techniques in these pages for stringing, creating nets, edging leather or fabric, finishing with a clasp, fashioning small free-form objects, shaping open bags and baskets, bead weaving on a loom, and making various decorative pins, pendants, key rings, earrings, necklaces, bracelets, and other ornaments of your own design. Besides the peyote stitch found in Chapters 4, 8, and 15, Chapters 10 to 16 also draw on various beading techniques to create more three-dimensional objects, such as bags, baskets, key rings, earrings,

pendants, and pins. Photo-copy and use the peyote stitch, brick stitch, or the loom or square-stitch graphs on pp. 119–121 to visualize the work, plan your color scheme, or create designs of your own.

People who do beadwork readily acknowledge that their beads "speak" to them. Beads are like letters that are merely abstract symbols for compos-ing words of human expres-sion. They form a universal language that appears to cross all cultures. We hope that the beadwork you see in these pages and out in the world will "speak" to you of history, culture, health, beauty, art, and spirituality.

BEAD THERAPY

Beads through the centuries have supported prayer and ceremony and ministered to spiritual needs. Beading also is naturally therapeu-tic, and in the last few decades, bead therapy has spread into com-munities across the United States and into many foreign countries.

Bead therapy has been helpful in cultural, after-school, day-care, and recreation programs. It is currently used in institutions as diverse as nursing homes for the elderly and prisons for long-term inmates. Many institutions serving psychiatric and medical needs have also discovered the healing effects of bead therapy. Patients in convalescent homes and hospices as well as those undergoing the torments of alcohol or drug-treatment programs find that beading and bead therapy, whether formal or informal, offer a kind a soothing reassurance.

2

SONORA-WEAVE CHOKER

The Sonora Desert is home to the Mohave, Yaqui, Mayo, Huichol, Yuma, Quechan, Tohono O'odham, Pima, Gila River, and other tribes. Many small tribes and clans also reside in the desert Southwest. Many different peoples from this region have made similar types of collars, necklaces, and even shawls using the vertical netting stitch. With so much intermarriage and global movement, it has become more and more difficult to identify where a given technique originated. This particular necklace was named to identify a region in southeast California, south Arizona, and northwest Mexico. Some evidence suggests that the technique may have originated in Africa.

- 1 tube or hank of size 11 black beads (about 1 ounce)

- 1 tube or hank of size 11 silver beads

- 1 tube or hank of size 11 yellow beads

- 1 tube or hank of size 11 orange beads

- 31 red teardrop-shaped beads, drilled from top to bottom

- 2 split rings (like miniature key rings)

- 1 clasp

- size B or O thread

- size 10 or 12 beading needle

- scissors

- clear nail polish

Project Notes: Although the more traditional beaded neck pieces were very ornate and worn for special occasions, the pattern here is for a simple choker-style necklace, worn by old and young alike. Once you master the technique, you can create your own elaborate piece of jewelry. The technique produces a very fluid bead fabric that conforms gracefully to the wearer's neckline. This particular necklace measures about 15½ inches long, including the clasp. By following the basic pattern and adding more rows, you can make a shoulder-length collar or over-the-shoulder shawl.

Colors and patterns can be significant, if the designer chooses. However, for the sake of simplicity, this pattern calls for only two colors, identified as a main color and a marker bead. The marker bead is a contrasting color that helps you know which bead to attach your netting to when you are adding rows of beadwork. At the bottom of the necklace are the sunset colors of yellow and orange seed beads ending with red teardrop-shaped beads.

1. Thread your needle with about 2 yards of double thread. Begin by picking up 8 main-color beads and one split ring on your needle. Tie the beads in a circle with a square knot. Reinforce the ring by going through all eight beads again with your needle and thread. Tie a square knot and glue with clear nail polish. Let it dry before trimming your thread. Use a half-hitch or in-line knot periodically to secure your work throughout the beadwork project.

2. The length of the necklace is strung horizontally. String 1 marker bead and 4 main-color beads to form a set of 5 beads.

3. Repeat the pattern until you reach about 15 inches, ending with a marker bead. If you need to increase or decrease the length, do it in sets of 5 beads. There are 51 bottom points in this necklace. An even number of marker beads will make an odd number of points. In the finished necklace there are exactly 31 teardrop beads with 10 plain-bottom points on each side, for a total of 51.

4. When you reach the end of the length of the necklace, string another set of 8 beads to make the ring for the other end of the clasp. Enclose the clasp before knotting. Reinforce the ring by passing your needle and thread through all 8 beads again and exiting through the last marker bead strung.

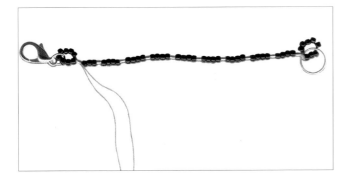

5. String the following pattern, which is going to be woven vertically: 3 main color, 1 marker, 3 main color, 1 marker, 3 main color, 1 marker, 3 main color (3–1–3–1–3–1–3).

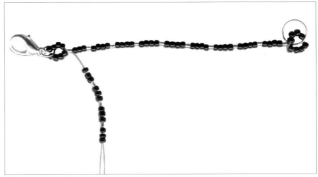

6. Pass your needle through the last marker bead strung, called a turnaround bead.

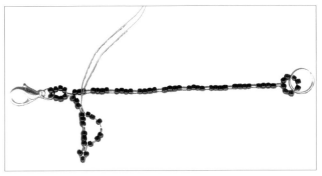

7. Add a set of 3–1–3 beads and pass your needle through the first marker bead strung.

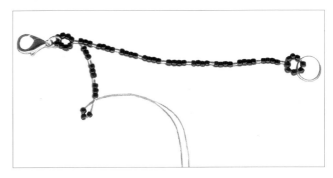

8. Add 3 more main-color beads and pass your needle through the second marker bead strung on the main part of the necklace, which was strung horizontally. This changes the direction of the thread path, which is now heading down.

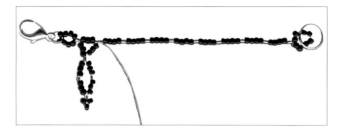

9. String 3–1–3 and pass the needle through the second marker bead from the previous row.

10. String 3–1–3 and make your turnaround. Continue with the same pattern until you have 10 bottom points. Then start adding your teardrop beads for your bottom turnaround. When you finish the length of the necklace, tie a secure knot, and glue with clear nail polish.

VARIATION

For a challenge, try making matching earrings. Experiment with your own colors and patterns to make an individual fashion statement. The earrings shown here with the Sonora-weave choker are made with a combination of techniques: Apache weave on the top (see Chapter 8) and Huichol netting on the bottom.

3

NETTED GOURD

Circular netting, horizontal netting, or Huichol lace

Beginner

Gourds, along with other organic products like corn, chiles, and feathers, are becoming increasingly popular for use in artistic projects. Gourds come in a variety of sizes and shapes. They are used for diverse projects, such as making ornaments, spoons, bowls, birdhouses, and numerous other decorative items. Ceremonially, they are used for rattles and musical percussion instruments. In fact, dried gourds are like natural rattles because the dried seeds inside make a soft rustling noise when shaken. To accentuate the noise, a dried gourd can be drilled and small pebbles or seeds inserted. Try filling your gourd with sand rubies, dried beans, gem chips, or even seed beads to appreciate the subtle sound differences. Gourds are often decorated with beads, leather, feathers, fetishes, seeds, shells, and charms. Whoever said that "art imitates nature" succinctly summed up the common view that the beauty found in nature is unsurpassed by anything made by human hands or machines. Our best artistic intentions pay homage to the awesome beauty we see in nature.

This netted gourd project uses cedar seeds for embellishment. Cedar is a tree well known for its distinctive smell. The leaf of the evergreen is used as a type of incense in American Indian ceremonies. The ethereal smoke symbolizes the healing prayers sent to the Creator. It is used as a cleansing agent that clears out negative energy and draws in positive energy. The essential oil contained in the plant has antibacterial qualities, so its cleansing effects may be more concrete than abstract. The seeds are often called ghost beads because of the association with the historically significant Ghost Dance.

Many beaded items found in museums are functional, ceremonial, or both. A Tarahumara artist renowned for wood carvings was asked about the spiritual significance of his bowl. He replied that it was made to hold beans, a humble food for a humble people. When he was asked further if it had any special meaning or symbolism, he responded that his prayer was to keep the bowl filled with food for his family. Whether he was being humorous, sarcastic, or simply straightforward is a matter of interpretation. The concept of what is sacred is a question we need to ask ourselves and live our lives accordingly.

The spiritual philosophy of many Native Americans revolves around living in harmony with nature. Their day-to-day activities with all the inherent mundane aspects of life are recognized as integral facets of their spiritual belief system. They demonstrate their respect for nature by using many natural items in a good way. Their artwork demonstrates their respect for nature by their efforts to enhance the beauty they see all around them. Look around and decide what is sacred to you.

- 2 colors (minimum) of seed beads, size 10, 11, 12, 13, or 14

- size B or D thread for larger beads

- size A or O thread for smaller beads. (Artificial sinew is strong enough for use with pony beads, size 6 or size 8 beads.)

- size 10 or 12 beading needle for seed beads

- big-eye needle for larger beads

- embellishment beads (We used drilled cedar seeds.)

- dried gourd

Project Notes: This netted gourd is embellished with other natural materials. The stitch is commonly called Huichol lace, named after the Huichol Indians of Mexico. It is a very useful technique for covering a three-dimensional object with beads. Netting is a forgiving stitch because it is flexible and adapts to the shape it is beaded around. Gourds are grown commercially for use by the art community. You can buy them directly from specialty farmers in rural areas or from retail outlets or online sources that carry arts and craft supplies. In the fall, some grocery stores even carry gourds for purchase. Since they are produced by nature, they are not all perfectly shaped or the same. Choose a good one that "speaks" to you.

We've used a small bilobal-shaped gourd, often called a peyote gourd. The technique of increasing and decreasing netting will help you learn how to cover any shape you need. The gourd in the photo (above right) is about 4 inches tall when standing. The round one is called a coyote gourd.

1. Begin by threading your needle with an arm's length (about 1 yard) of thread. Starting at the top of the gourd, string enough beads to make a ring around the stem in sets of 3 beads (2 main color and 1 marker bead). A small gourd will usually accommodate 5 or 6 sets.

Tie the ring with a square knot and secure with clear nail polish. Reinforce the ring by passing your needle and thread all the way around the ring again and tie off with a half-hitch knot. Move your needle so that it exits a marker bead.

2. String a set of 3–1–3 (3 main-color beads, 1 marker bead, and 3 main-color beads) and pass your needle through the next marker bead.

3. Continue adding sets of 3–1–3 until you have reached the first marker bead. At the end of each row, tie a half-hitch knot to secure your tension. You do this by passing your needle under the thread, creating a loop. Pass your needle through the loop to make a half-hitch or in-line knot.

4. Pass your needle through the first set you added, exiting the middle marker bead. This step brings you down to begin the next row or level.

5. Increase by 1 every row until you reach the widest part of the gourd. The next row you will be adding a set of 4–1–4 from marker bead to marker bead. The following row will be 5–1–5. Don't forget to tie a half-hitch or in-line knot at the end of each row to hold the tension while you are covering the gourd.

6. Continue increasing until you reach the widest part of the gourd and then begin to decrease. You decrease by reducing the number of beads in each set. If the widest row is made with sets of 10–1–10, then decrease to 9–1–9, and then 8–1–8 until the gourd is completely covered. Don't be afraid to improvise by trial and error to get a good fit.

7. Do not glue your knots until you are finished with the embellishments because the nail polish on the knots can plug the bead hole. One bead may have to accommodate several passes of thread if you add beaded fringe, loops, fetishes, or other embellishments.

VARIATION

In the gourd in the project, loops of beads and cedar seeds are added to form a type of skirting effect on the gourd. Dyed red leather was braided around the stem. The cedar seeds brush against the outside of the gourd to make a gentle rattling sound.

Sea shells, feathers, leather, horsehair, seeds, nuts, porcupine quills, and beads of stone, clay, bones, cork, and wood are examples of the types of organic embellishments that can be used to decorate gourds. This beaded gourd (photo right), created by Shelia Vinson, uses gemstone bear fetishes and silver feathers for embellishment.

4

FLORAL BRACELET

Flat peyote stitch

Intermediate

People all over the world love flowers because of their delicate petals, lovely shapes, vibrant colors, and fragrance. For the Yoeme people of the Sonoran Desert, flowers have special significance. Flowers decorate their altars and hold a prominent place in ceremonies and beliefs.

The Yoeme's sea ania, roughly translated as "the flower world," is a pre-Christian concept of all of nature in bloom. Even water in nature, rivers, streams, lakes, clouds, and rain are expressed in flowers and grow fruitful. Local people describe nature in a contemporary and real sense, but realize the presence of supernatural essence. The flower world refers to a place of enchantment originating from the ancient world. Some feel that the smell of roses can transport you into the beauty of the flower world.

The word flower, or sewa, can be translated as "sacred" or "holy." It symbolizes life and beauty, harmony with nature, goodness, blessings, heavenly rewards, good deeds, and the supernatural world. It is likened to the concept of heaven on earth where deer roam freely and humans live in harmony with nature.

This particular pattern comes from a lovely Tohono O'odham woman, Delphine, who has six delightful children. She found this pattern deep in her memory from her own childhood.

- 1 tube size 11 background color beads (We used black.)
- 1 tube size 11 for each flower color
- 2 split rings (like a miniature key ring)
- 1 clasp
- 1 size 10 or 12 beading needle
- 1 spool size B, O, or A thread

Project Notes: This bracelet pattern is a favorite of children and beginners. Generally, children ages seven to nine seem to have excellent dexterity, hand-eye coordination, and visual acuity for this type of beadwork. Their minds are open and their creativity is intact. Therefore, it is a great age to begin learning beadwork.

Although the finished appearance is similar, this technique is quite different from what is commonly referred to as a daisy chain. The daisy chain usually consists of a flower pattern in linear sequence, but this pattern has flowers alternating from side to side.

This bracelet is made with four beads across the width of the bracelet. When you learn how to do the flat peyote stitch, the pattern can be easily adapted to make a wider bracelet or amulet bag strap. The basic pattern can also be used to make a necklace or ankle bracelet. The easiest method of flat peyote stitch is to use an even number of beads, often referred to as even-count peyote stitch.

Who knew that such a simple piece of beadwork could hold such powerful symbolism? While working on this beaded flower bracelet, think of each flower as a blessing.

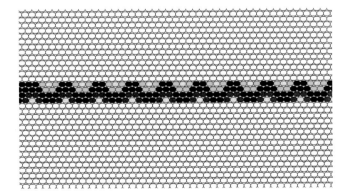

1. Tie a bead at the end of your thread so that your beads won't fall off. This is called a stop bead. String four beads, using the background color.

2. Pick up a fifth bead (same color), skip a bead, and pass your needle through the next bead.

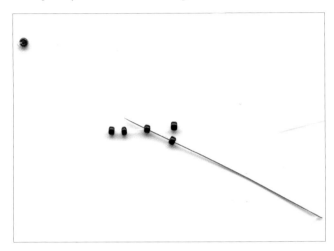

3. Pick up another background bead and pass it through the last bead, closest to the stop bead.

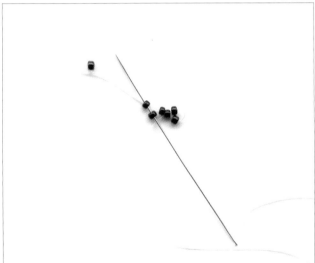

Peyote stitch actually adds only half a row at a time, so on your next row you will be adding only two beads. You will be adding one bead every other bead in one direction and then adding one bead every other bead in the opposite direction (alternating right to left and then left to right).

4. At this point, your beads should line up just like the picture. Tie a square knot with your main thread and your thread tail to stabilize the beadwork. Glue the knot with clear nail polish.

5. You will now be picking up a flower bead and passing your needle through the bead that sticks out, often called a pop-up bead.

6. Your next bead added will be a background color bead.

7. Follow the pattern until your needle exits the top flower bead.

8. Pick up two flower beads and pass your needle through the bottom flower bead.

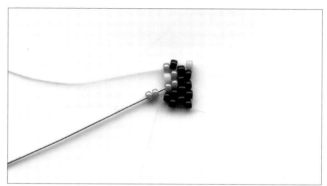

9. Pass your needle all around the flower beads until your needle exits the top flower bead. Continue beading with flat peyote stitch, following the pattern to place your alternating flowers. Notice that the top of one flower is on the same row as the bottom of the next flower.

10. When your bracelet is the appropriate length (7½ inches is average, including the clasp), add a loop of 8 beads and the clasp hardware on each end. Reinforce the loop at least two times with your thread and weave your thread back a few inches into your bracelet.

11. Knot securely and glue with clear nail polish. After it dries, trim the thread tail.

VARIATION

The photo shows the same pattern in Delicas, which are smaller than size 11 beads. The two side beads of each flower are left off, which changes the appearance of the bracelet. It features a magnetic clasp, which is very comfortable and easy to use.

BONE-HAIR-PIPE BRACELET

The origin of the term bone hair pipe, *also referred to as* bone hairpipe, *describes a type of tubular bead made of bone or shell. They are typically seen in modern dance regalia such as breastplates and chokers. These beads are a vestige of a functional aspect of battle dress that protected the chest and vital organs from lethal injury during battle. The weapons of those days were bows and arrows. In modern times, bone-hair-pipe ornamentation is usually seen in dance costumes and competitions rather than on the battlefield. Dancers who wear them typically describe the chokers and breastplates as a sort of spiritual armor rather than a physical shield from injury. The bead itself is tubular in shape and has had a resurgence of popularity among natives and non-natives alike.*

- I tube of size 8 silver beads

- 9 bone-hair-pipe beads 1 inch long (other tubular beads can be substituted)

- 6 spacer bars with 3 holes each

- 8 to 10 inches of turquoise gem chips

- 6 fire-polish beads 6 to 8 mm

- 2 pieces of 30 inches long stringing

- wire 0.18 to 0.20 gauge

- 10 crimper beads

- crimper tool or flat-nose pliers

- 6 horn beads (can be substituted with bone or glass beads)

- 1 silver button or concho

3. Put all four ends of wire through 1 crimper bead and slide up the wires for a snug fit. Slip it over the concho or button to make sure it fits and add or subtract beads accordingly.

Project Notes: This bracelet project is made with turquoise chips, glass fire-polish beads, bone-hair-pipe beads, horn-disk beads, bone and horn spacer bars, and silver glass beads strung on nylon-coated wire cable. The traditional method of assembly involved the use of animal sinew, which is now replaced with artificial sinew. The artificial product is made of nylon or polyester fibers that have been waxed. The spacer bars are sometimes made of metal or leather. The glass fire-polish beads are fired at a high temperature to produce smooth instead of sharp facets and a luscious finish. The clasp is a simple loop designed to attach a silver concho or button. A concho is a concave piece of silver that is stamped and has a welded button shank. The chokers are frequently seen with an abalone button attached in the middle with leather ties.

1. Cut 2 pieces of stringing wire 30 inches each.

2. Place about 24 size 8 beads onto both wires and gently fold in half without kinking the wire.

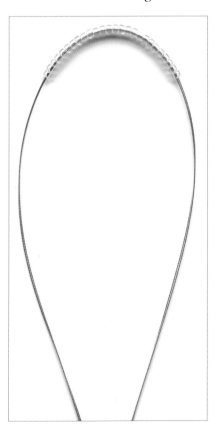

4. With a crimper tool or flat-nose pliers, gently apply pressure to flatten the crimper bead and hold it in place. Try tugging on the bead to make sure it is held in place securely. If it moves, apply pressure with your tool again.

5. Cut the extra piece of wire with wire cutters so that you only have 3 wires to string. You are now ready to begin stringing. It is easiest to lay out your pattern on a bead board or table to make sure that it looks appealing and will have a custom fit. The average bracelet length is about 7½ inches long, including the clasp.

6. If you are satisfied with the design and length, string the other two pieces of beading wire.

7. String 3 size 8 beads and 1 crimper bead at the end of each wire. String each wire through the shank of the button or concho and back through the crimper bead. Weave your tail back through an inch or so of the body of the bracelet.

8. One at a time, gently pull on the tail of each wire so that it is snug before you crimp it with the crimping tool. Don't pull your wires so tight that the bracelet buckles. It should fit comfortably, not stiffly, on your wrist. Don't forget to test your crimp to make sure that it is secure.

9. Trim off excess wire with wire cutters.

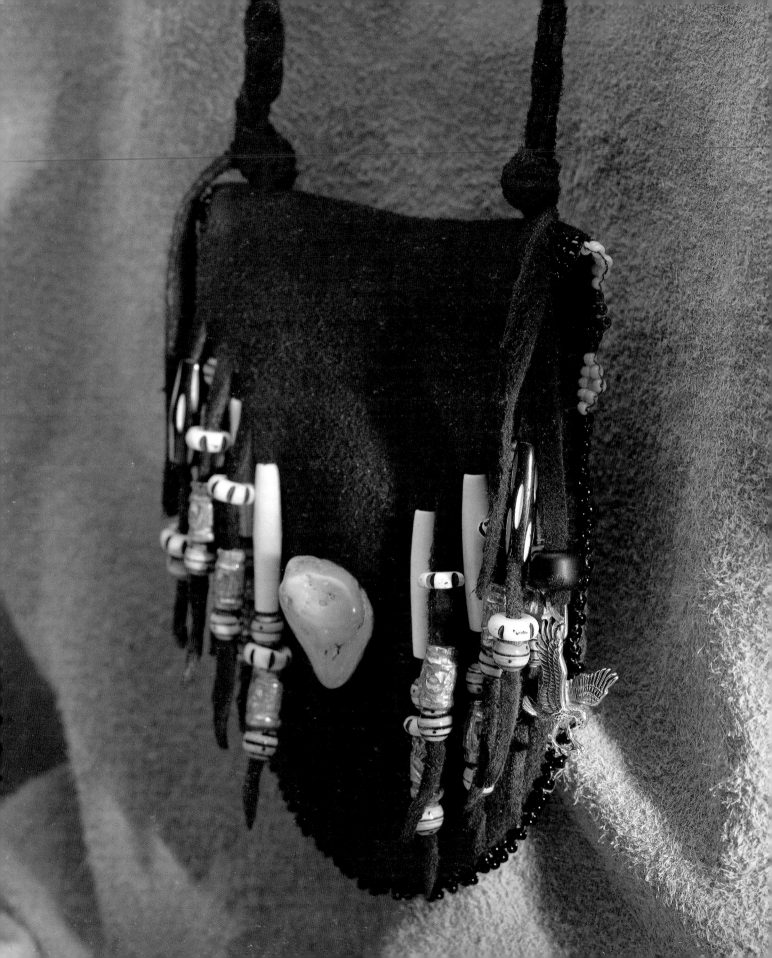

6

LEATHER MEDICINE BAG

To describe the function of a medicine bag is to understand the meaning of medicine ascribed to by the person making or wearing it. Traditionally, a medicine bag is made by the individual wearer or given as a gift to someone special. A medicine bag is very personal because of its meaning and the symbolism of the colors, designs, fetishes, and ultimately, its contents. Medicine bags are frequently worn inside a person's clothing, around the neck, or tucked inside the waistband. However, a fancy one can also be worn in public or during ceremonies. Contemporary uses include holding such contents as healing herbs, pharmaceuticals, gemstones, fetishes, prayer beads, or any article of special significance.

This particular leather medicine bag was made for my daughter, who was traveling overseas. A great deal of thought, planning, and prayers went into the bag. Therefore, its details provide an example of some of the many uses of a medicine bag. First, the bag was made of red leather because that's her favorite color and it symbolizes life and all its passions. She is a young woman facing a tremendous adventure with courage and excitement, but also with a bit of trepidation because of the lengthy time she'll spend away from her family and friends. So the bag helps her face this distance and fear of the unknown.

The colors of the seed beads used for the edging are black, white, red, and yellow, sacred colors representing the four human races and the four directions. Since she was leaving to study with international students from around the globe, it served as a reminder to recognize that all peoples are created the same regardless of their perceived differences. One of my favorite prayers is a simple expression translated to "we are all related" or "all my relations." It is a concise philosophy promoting harmony with other people and all of nature.

My daughter wanted her medicine bag to be decorated with turquoise. The relevance of turquoise is that the beautiful blue stone resembling the sky and water was given to the native peoples to remind them that they hold special favor. This notion is comparable to a father telling each of his many children that each child is his favorite. The object is to encourage an individual to feel a close personal relationship with his father and making them feel good, special, and reassured. Turquoise is recognized throughout the world as the stone of love and friendship.

She also requested that her bag be decorated with bone-hair-pipe beads, remnants of the former shell or foundation of spirits long gone to the other world. Metaphorically, the bones of the earth embody the heavy yet translucent burden that rests on the spirit. Bone beads typically seen in Native American arts and crafts are usually made of bovine bones, such as those from a cow, ox, or water buffalo. They are natural and organic beads still used in spite of the availability of beads manufactured with sophisticated technology, like those made of glass, faceted gemstones, or metal beads that are precision cut with machines and lasers.

She also chose hand-painted ceramic beads that looked to her like a landscape of the painted desert with glorious sunset colors. For a bit of contrast, the bag also contains handcrafted pewter-face beads.

All items mentioned so far are clearly visible on the outside of the bag. The contents inside the bag are typically unseen, but we'll let you know what's inside and explain their significance. First, my daughter expressed some apprehension of experiencing homesickness, which can manifest itself in physical as well as psychological symptoms. An elderly American Indian woman advised me on a cure for such an ailment. She explained that her son was having some problems with homesickness when he was serving his time overseas in the military. She sent him some dirt from their home to literally "ground" him and remind him of who he was and where he came from. This technique was apparently quite effective, so my daughter's bag holds some earth from my herb garden to remind her of home and, we hope, to prevent the uncomfortable longings for familiarity.

She also told me that two things in particular reminded her of home: the smell of freshly brewed coffee and the smoke of the herb sage, so both of these items were included. Olfactory memory and associations are potent psychological tools for regaining emotional balance. Although coffee is not typically considered a sacred herb, the value of an object is derived from an individual's experiences and associations. Sage is used ceremonially to cleanse and purify or to bless one's self and eliminate negative influences. Many people describe the smell of burning sage as heavenly.

Also included in her bag is a turtle fetish made of clay. This is to remind her of this great continent called Turtle Island, which is where she was born, where she belongs, and where she will return when she is done with her travels.

Since humans are not able to fly naturally, we rely on the spirit of winged creatures, so a silver-eagle fetish was included to remind her to have keen vision and to focus on the important things in life. With this bag, I prayed for her safe airplane travel, a wonderful adventure, and a safe return.

- I square foot of soft, thin leather (12×12 inches)

- sharp leather or fabric scissors

- white glue

- leather hole puncher or ice pick

- 3 strands of leather lace measuring 28 inches each or waxed cotton cord

- embellishment beads, charms, and fetishes

- size 10 beading needle

- size O or B beading thread

- 4 colors of size 11 seed beads

Project Notes: This medicine bag is made with leather cut in the shape of the pattern as shown. Substitutes for leather are Ultrasuede® or similar fabrics that do not fray. Fairly thin leather is recommended because the beading needle must be able to sew onto the fabric as well as to accommodate the bead size. The size of the finished bag is about 5 inches high by 3 inches wide, not including the strap.

1. Using the pattern (templates) on pages 122 and 123, cut out two pieces of leather. For a bag with a flap, cut one of A and one of B. For the smaller bag, cut out two of pattern C. (If you photocopy the templates, you can then cut out the paper and pin it on top of your leather or other fabric.)

2. Glue the wrong sides together by putting a thin line of white glue on the shorter piece about ½ inch away from the edge. This serves to hold the pieces in place temporarily while you sew the beads onto the edge.

3. Thread your needle with about 2 yards of thread and tie a knot on the end. Pass your needle and thread through one edge of leather between the two pieces to conceal the knot.

4. Pick up 3 beads and pass your needle through the front side only about 1 bead-width away from your thread as shown.

5. Turning your leather work over, run your needle through the edge of the fabric and up through the last 2 beads added.

6. Continue by adding 3 beads, stitch through the front layer only, turn your work over and come up the last 3 beads added.

Continue adding beads in the following pattern for each color, 1–2–3–2–1.

7. The edging shown so far is called a scallop stitch. The edging stitch shown at the bottom of the bag is more commonly called fretting. It is the same basic stitch except that you pick up 2 beads, stitch into the front of the bag, and come back up only 1 bead. There are many variations of this stitch based on the number of beads you stack.

8. After you have finished the beaded edge, punch 2 holes through both thickness of leather for adding the strap. Thin leather strips were braided and tied together with an overhand knot. A substitute for the leather strap is a thin piece of waxed cotton cord or a beaded strap as shown in Chapter 4. A beaded strap can be attached directly onto the leather without punching holes.

9. With sharp scissors or leather shears, cut the fringe on the flap of the bag and decorate it with big-hole beads. You will notice that soft leather tends to stretch, which is why the fringe on the edges is longer than the short fringe in the middle.

10. Use a dot of white glue or leather cement to hold the fringe beads in place. If you are adding a gemstone or cabochon, use jewelry or leather cement. It is wise to test the glue on a piece of scrap leather to make sure that it is not too stiff, which could ruin the beauty of the supple leather. Epoxy glues are not recommended because they become brittle with age and lose their holding power.

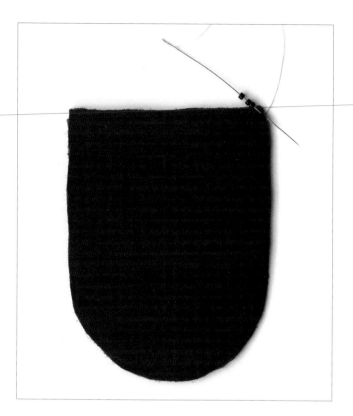

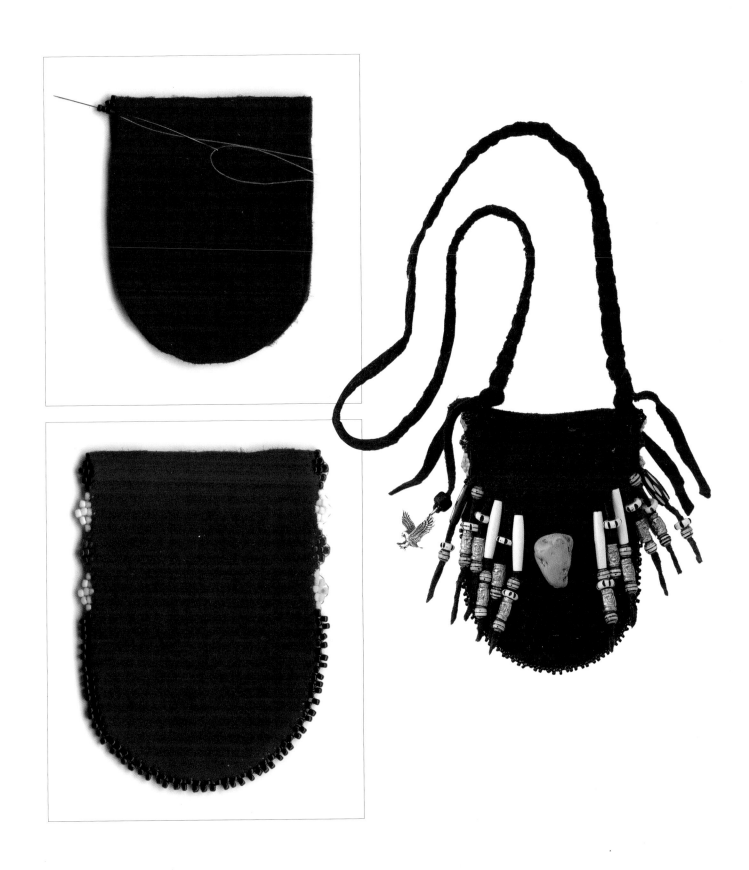

7

TRIPLE-STRAND FETISH NECKLACE

This necklace uses a relatively easy technique of bead stringing, but the resulting piece of jewelry is both elegant and striking. This particular piece is styled after the pueblo heishe jewelry. In New Mexico seventeen small villages, called pueblos, are home to many different clans of Native Americans. The term heishe (pronounced he-she) refers to a very old style of making beads from shell and gemstone chips, such as turquoise. The chips are individually drilled by hand and then strung on sinew or cord. They are then rolled to wear down the chips into a smooth strand of beads. It is a very arduous and lengthy process. The smooth beads are then used to make different types of jewelry by adding silver findings, gem chips, and hand-carved fetishes.

The necklace in the photo actually uses glass seed beads from the Czech Republic, which simulate the natural color blends of shell heishe. American Indian hand-made rolled heishe is very rare and expensive. For the tourist trade, beaders often import heishe from the Philippines. The fetishes used may symbolize certain characteristics of the animal after which it is modeled. Bear fetishes are extremely popular and symbolize strength, stamina, and healing.

The glass beads are accented with assorted gemstone fetishes and amber chips. Because of access to markets around the world, many types of beads, gems, and fetishes, are more readily available to the modern jewelry maker. By making your own jewelry, you can make lovely pieces more affordable, and importing heishe means a lot less time and labor invested.

- I hank or I tube of size 10 or 11 seed beads (Pre-blended color mixes are available, but if you can't find them at your favorite bead store, choose 3 to 4 colors in the same family and blend your own.)

- about 30 fetishes

- I strand of gemstone chips, about 12 inches

- size 4 pearl knotting cord (You can substitute size D or F bead thread as along as the stringing material is strong enough to hold the weight of the fetishes and gem chips.)

- 2 eye pins

- 2 silver cones ¾ inch in length

- clasp

- big-eye needle (Packaged beading cord comes with a twisted-wire needle attached.)

- beading board or a tape measure

- white glue

- round needle-nose pliers

- cutting pliers

- scissors

Project Notes: This necklace consists of three strands of beads mixed with amber chips and assorted gemstone fetishes. They are each strung separately in 20-inch lengths. If you would prefer to make a graduated length necklace, try making the longest strand 22 inches long, not including the added length of the clasp; the middle strand 20 inches long; and the short strand 18 inches long. Finish off the necklace with sterling silver cones and clasp. The length can be altered to suit your taste. However, most prepackaged pearl knotting cord comes in approximately 6-foot lengths, so if you make the triple-strand necklace longer than suggested in this project, you may need more knotting cord.

1. String your first strand of beads, mixed with fetishes and gem chips, to a length of 20 inches. A beading board is very useful for beginners because the layout helps you see how it will look. If you don't use a beading board, use a tape measure or ruler to determine the length. If you are not sure, hold the first strand up to your neck to see how it hangs and whether it is long enough to suit your taste. A piece of masking tape or a stop bead at the end of the cord will prevent the beads from falling off while you are working.

2. String two more strands, each 20 inches long.

3. Gather the three ends of the cord and thread through the eye of the eye pin.

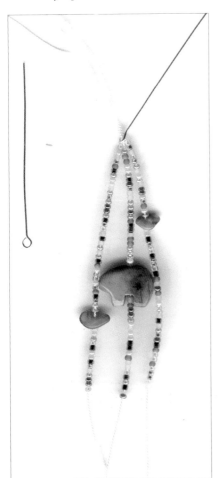

4. Tie a half-hitch knot around the neck of the eye pin.

5. Tie an extra knot if necessary to make it secure. Put white glue on the knot and set aside to dry.

6. Tie off the other end of the necklace the same way.

7. When the glue is dry, trim the excess cord.

8. Slide the cone over the eye pin and tug gently so that no cord shows.

9. Trim both eye pins to about ½ inch.

10. With your round needle-nose pliers, bend the wire into a ring, leaving enough room to slip one end of the clasp over the ring and close it. Finish adding the other end of the clasp.

Some people like to twist the
strands of the necklace to give it
a fuller look.

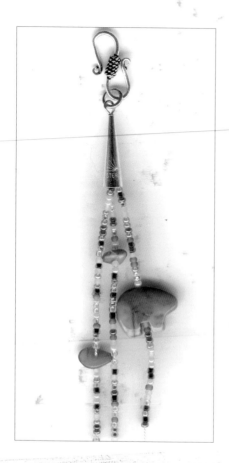

VARIATIONS

*The photo shows two examples of heishe
necklaces. A Santo Domingo pueblo woman
who was selling her jewelry at a Santa Fe
flea market in New Mexico made the
long necklace, strung with real
pen-shell heishe and assorted gemstone chips. The short choker style
necklace (shown extreme right) is
made with turquoise and shell.*

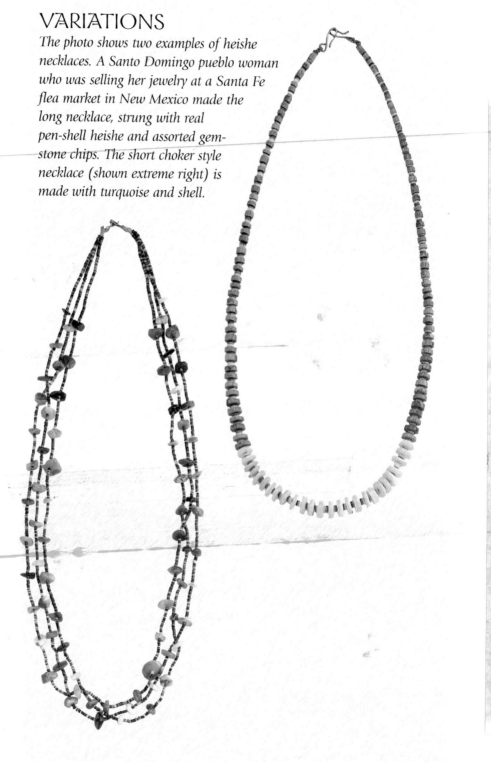

8

BEAR EARRINGS

The bear is one of the most powerful Native American symbols. Many tribes use it to symbolize strength, protection, and healing. Bear clan members associate the bear's spirit with a powerful force of nature that brings with it a sense of wisdom, honesty, and social responsibility. Jonathan Michael Pulley, my son, designed the small bear featured in this pattern.

The bear spirit is one of moral authority and righteousness. It is also a spirit of good health and healing when the human body and spirit encounter sickness. An elderly medicine man told me a creation story about the bear as being one of humans' closest relatives. He said that the bear was divinely ordained to teach us all we need to know about healing plants that were created on earth for the benefit of all humans. The bear is a powerful ally in many respects.

We need to consider the cultural context to define the meaning of native symbols. Vast cultural differences are seen among the tribes if we attempt to ascribe the powers of various animal fetishes. The artist's relationship with animal fetishes is necessarily very personal and grows from the artist's individual experiences. The artist is the first line of authority in describing his or her artwork and its meaning. However, artists themselves are also defined by their social, cultural, tribal, clan, and family memberships.

Traditionally, the artist was more likely involved in embellishing utilitarian or ceremonial objects rather than in art for art's sake. The artist in our modern society typically has more time to devote to creative expression, within the realm of day-to-day life experiences. Many young artists, especially beaders, are drawn to the tourist trade to make money and to receive acknowledgement for developing fine motor and artistic skills. Therefore, a primary motivation for an aspiring artist is to produce items, colors, or symbols that are popular in the retail market. Many traditional designs and patterns are complex, both symbolically and in the effort involved to produce them.

In addition, Native American art and its design elements have been widely imitated worldwide. If imitation is viewed as the highest form of compliment, then one must concede that the world loves native art! Therefore, the best advice to buyers of beadwork is to identify the artist and, if possible, to ask him or her directly about the meaning of his or her artwork. On the other hand, if a tourist item is aesthetically appealing as an object of personal adornment or art, then buy it and enjoy it!

- 2 to 3 colors of Japanese cylinder beads

- size 10 needle

- size A or O beading thread

- ear wires

- accent beads for the fringe (optional, such as 3 to 4 mm fire-polish beads, bugle beads, crystals, porcupine quills, turquoise beads, gem chips, or pony beads)

Project Notes: This project is a pair of earrings made out of Delica beads, also known as cylinder beads. This type of bead is manufactured in Japan and extremely popular among beaders. The stitch is called Apache or Comanche weave; in other circles it may be referred to as brick stitch.

This type of earring is very common to the tourist trade, since many visitors to the Southwest American Indian country want a small souvenir of native arts and crafts. Younger women tend to prefer earrings with dangles or fringe as long as 3 to 4 inches, while older women tend to prefer this type of earring only 1 to 1½ inches long.

Typically, these earrings are seen in every color of the rainbow, but most often opaque colors. With the recent boom in the bead industry and competition between producers from Japan and the Czech Republic, many different types of seed beads, colors, and finishes are more available throughout the world. Glass beads are also produced in France and Italy. Although this particular pair of earrings is made with Japanese cylinder beads, almost every bead type and size is suitable. Uniformity is a key element in the neat appearance of beadwork. While deciding on beads for a project, remember to select all the colors from the same type and size of bead. When considering the sizing of beads, the smaller the size, the larger the beads. By the same token, the larger the bead size, the smaller the bead. Unfortunately, bead manufacturers do not maintain uniform standards and sizes all over the world.

The beginning row of this type of earring is usually made with a ladder stitch or a base row of bugle beads. This pattern begins with a 2-bead base row of flat peyote stitch, since it is easier and more stable. The resulting beadwork looks identical. Here we're creating earrings, but this beadwork can be used as a necklace pendant or beadwork pieces sewed onto a medicine bag, clothing, or moccasins. The bear image can also be incorporated into a beaded amulet bag, split-loom necklace, or other beaded object, like a lighter case or key ring.

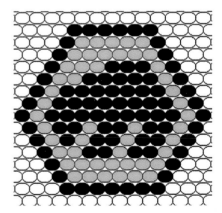

Reprinted by permission of Jonathan M. Pulley

1. Begin by threading about 1 yard of thread. Read your pattern by beginning at the widest part of the pattern. There are 13 beads across the widest part of the pattern. Place 2 black beads and a turquoise bead on your needle. Run your needle back through the first black bead to form a triangle.

2. With your 2 pieces of thread, tie a square knot and seal with a small dot of clear nail polish.

3. You will now continue adding beads with a flat peyote stitch. See Chapter 4 for more details. Adding only 1 bead at a time, pick up a turquoise bead and pass your needle through the pop-out turquoise bead. Changing directions with each bead added, continue beading the 2-bead base row, according to the graph shown above. The photo shows the first 2 rows completed.

4. Begin each row with 2 beads, in this case a black bead and a turquoise bead. From back to front, pass your needle under the second thread bridge (the little piece of thread showing between the second and third bead). Go up the second bead added and then down the first bead added. Then, come back up the second bead again. This step is called the up-down-up thing.

5. For the rest of the row, pick up one bead at a time. Put your needle under the thread bridge from back to front and then go back through the last bead you just added.

6. This technique decreases by one bead with every row. When you have finished the top half of the bear pattern, turn your work upside down and finish the bottom half. Add the earring loop by stringing 6 beads from the third bead to the fourth bead, attaching the ear wire in the middle. Reinforce the loop at least twice to secure the ear wire and then weave your thread to the base row to continue the bottom half of the pattern.

7. When you are done with the bear pattern, add the fringe by weaving your thread to the bottom row and exit the first bead. String 10 seed beads, 1 accent bead, and 3 seed beads. Skip the last 3 beads added (called turn-around beads) and run your needle back through all the other beads of your first fringe.

8. To add your next fringe, change directions by running your needle up through the first bead and down the second bead of the last row. Continue adding fringe the same way. Increase each fringe by 2 beads until you reach the middle fringe and then start to decrease by 2 beads. In the picture shown above right, the number of beads in the fringe is strung according to the following pattern: 10–12–14–16–14–12–10. You can easily change the length of your earrings by altering the number of beads per fringe.

9. Finally, make another one just like it if you are traditional and like wearing matching earrings. Get creative and try making a matching necklace pendant. Experiment with color patterns in the fringe and use different-colored bead combinations to make more bear earrings.

VARIATION

Here's another example of the same stitch, beaded by Judy Gorman.

COMANCHE-
WEAVE FEATHER

Comanche weave

Advanced

This simple little beaded feather can be used in many different types of beadwork projects, such as earrings, charms, hat pins, tie tacks, collar pins, and fringe for bags.

The beaded feathers also look great as embellishment on leather bags. This feather was made with Japanese cylinder beads (also called Delicas) and measures about 1 inch long. These feathers also look nice when made with larger beads.

The technique is named after two different American Indian tribes, the Comanche and the Apache, known for their skill as warriors. The Comanche or Apache weave is also known as the brick stitch.

The eagle feather itself is a powerful symbol, given to people as recognition of an accomplishment or to acknowledge a noteworthy feat. In the book The Sacred Pipe, Black Elk describes why the Spotted Eagle and his feathers are considered sacred. Black Elk writes that the eagle is an animal that flies the highest of all creatures and sees everything.

He is a solar bird and his feathers are compared to the rays of the sun. When an eagle feather is carried or worn, the individual identifies with the eagle's spiritual or sacred being.

- 1 tube black Delicas
- 1 tube white Delicas
- other colors (your choice) for the feather body
- size A or O beading thread
- size 12 or 10 beading needle
- clear nail polish
- scissors
- findings, such as ear wires, stick pin, tie tack, or pin back, depending on the project

Project Notes: This beaded feather uses a pattern of increasing and decreasing rows to give the feather its shape. The feather is beaded from the bottom to the top. The top can be finished off with a bead loop to attach an ear wire or split ring to give the feather some fluidity of movement to use as a charm or pendant. It is easy to adapt the pattern to make the feather wider or longer.

1. Tie 3 beads into a triangle and secure with a knot. The triangle is at the bottom of the feather pattern and forms rows 1 and 2. Refer to the pattern to see what colors you need to select.

4. The next row is an increase row, which means that it has more beads than the previous row. Pick up two beads and pass your needle under the thread bridge, as shown. (The thread bridge is the little piece of thread showing between 2 beads.) Pass your needle from the bottom "up" the red bead you just added, "down" the black bead you just added, and then back "up" the red bead. Add one more black bead by going under the same thread bridge and back up through the bead you just added.

5. The next two rows are also increase rows. Just follow the pattern on the graph to know which color of bead to pick up. Remember, we are following the pattern from the bottom tip of the feather and working up. Pick up 2 beads at the beginning of each row, pass your needle under the thread bridge, and do the up-down-up thing described in step 4. The first five rows are increase rows.

2. Seal the knot with a dot of clear nail polish.

3. Move the thread over one bead with your needle to get your thread tail out of the way. Wait until the nail polish is thoroughly dry before trimming.

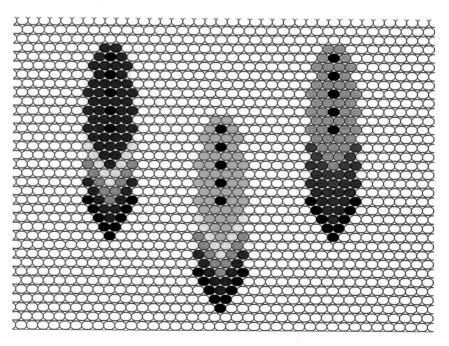

6. When you reach the sixth row, you will decrease by picking up 2 beads and passing your needle under the second thread bridge. Do the up-down-up thing and finish the row by adding one bead at a time by going under each thread bridge and through the bead.

7. Continue following the pattern until you finish the top 2-bead row. For earrings, add 6 beads to form a loop coming out of the last row of beads and attach an ear wire. Reinforce at least three times and tie a secure knot. Weave your thread into the body of the feather and tie off again. Use clear nail polish to secure the knot. Let it dry thoroughly before trimming your thread.

VARIATIONS

For a challenge, you can make the quill part of the feather solid by using a corn stitch. See Chapter 11 for detailed instructions on the stitch. These beaded feathers can be used as embellishments on many different types of projects, including earrings, tie tacks, collar tips, hat pins, necklaces, amulet bags, and hair ornaments.

10

CHILE PEPPER

Log cabin stitch; three-dimensional stacking stitch

Advanced

The technique used to make chile peppers is a rather unusual three-dimensional stitch that makes an object with a back, front, and two sides. The same stitch is seen on beaded animals like alligators, lizards, turtles, and frogs imported from South America, but the exact origins are not known.

Chile peppers are a very hot icon in the Southwest art world because they symbolize so much of the culture and natural beauty found in Arizona and New Mexico. The Native American, Spanish, and Anglo cultures have all learned to appreciate the intense gift of nature provided as food, spice, medicine, and artistic décor.

Foods including chile peppers that contain capsaicin cause the human brain to release endorphins into the system. An endorphin is any of a group of peptide hormones that bind to opiate receptors, found mainly in the brain. Endorphins reduce the sensation of pain and affect emotions. An endorphin is also a brain chemical occurring naturally in humans and having analgesic properties. The human brain's reaction to chiles is similar to its reaction to opium, sex, and love. Such a food must be seen as a gift from the heavens.

Medicinally, chiles are used as an ingredient in skin ointments for cold feet and sore muscles. Chile peppers are also used to treat high blood pressure, lethargy, and digestive problems. Their antiinflammatory properties are helpful in dealing with the symptoms of arthritis. Some people just like the taste of them and testify to their stimulating effects on appetite.

Chile plants are believed to have originated in South America. The Chile Pepper Institute at New Mexico State University in Las Cruces, New Mexico, is devoted to chile research. The mere existence of such organizations make people realize exactly how important the plant and fruit is to many people of different races and backgrounds throughout the world. Contact the institute for more information about chiles, descriptions of their nutrients, anatomy, cultivars, and growing information.

In the recent past, chile products were in high demand for home decorations and art projects, such as chile wreaths and ristras (strands of dried chile). Chiles appear in many tourist trinkets, like salsa dishes, shot glasses, Christmas lights, pot holders, and place mats. Some farmers claim that they sell more chile peppers to the art industry than the food industry.

Known for their phallic symbolism, a variety popular in New Mexico is an Anaheim chile pepper named Big Jim. Some chile varieties have pedigrees that rival the European monarchies. People like them for their flavor, heat, and colors, which include, yellow, green, red, black, and purple. Chile peppers used in jewelry designs reflect the celebration of the fall harvest and wonderful memories of food, family, and friends.

- pendant
- 2 to 3 colors size 6 to 8 pony beads
- 3 yards artificial sinew (split)
- tapestry needle or big-eye needle
- white glue

Project Notes: This beaded chile pepper* is a versatile component in jewelry making and home decorating. It is a three-dimensional stitch not commonly seen in beadwork. It is made with larger pony beads and used as a necklace pendant, key-ring pendant, fan pull, or decoration for a Christmas tree or wreath. When made with smaller beads, they are used as earrings and charms on a necklace, amulet bag, or bracelet. It is easier to learn the technique with bigger beads and then to try making the pattern with smaller beads, like size 11, Delicas, or size 14 beads. All other uses for the beaded chile peppers, like earrings or embellishment charms, require the necessary hardware, like ear wires, split rings, a key ring, or a floral wire to attach to the wreaths.

1. Thread your needle and string 6 beads as shown. Tie into a ring with a square knot, leaving a tail, which can be trimmed later.

2. Secure knot with white glue.

3. Run your needle through 3 beads and attach a side bead.

4. Run your needle through 3 more beads and add another side bead.

In this three-dimensional chile pepper, the beads are stacked up like a log cabin. First, you add the side beads, then the top beads and then the bottom beads.

5. After adding the side beads, add 4 top beads from 1 side bead to the other side bead.

6. Add 4 bottom beads through one side and then pass your needle through the four top beads. Continue the pattern as shown, adding side beads, then top beads, then the bottom beads. If your top beads and bottom beads are both the same color, it is easier to follow the pattern. Notice that the illustration is two-dimensional and the beaded chile is three-dimensional.

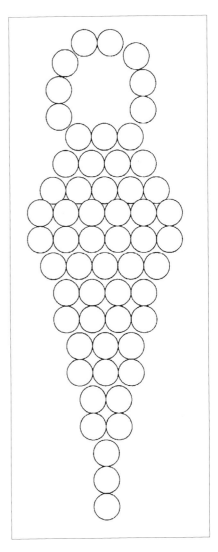

7. Add 5 bottom, through 1 side.

8. Add 5 top, through 1 side and 5 bottom.

9. Add 1 side through 5 top.

10. Add 1 side through 5 bottom and 1 side.

11. Add 6 top, through 1 side.

12. Add 6 bottom, through 1 side and 6 top.

13. Add 1 side, through 6 bottom.

14. Add 1 side, through 6 top and 1 side.

The number of beads per row is: 3–4–5–6–6–5–4–4–3–3–2–2–1–1–1.

Continue following the pattern until you have reached the tip of the chile pepper. Finish it off by adding one more side color bead on the bottom.

15. Knot securely and glue with white glue.

16. Finish the top by adding 6 to 8 beads from side to side for the chile-pepper stem.

VARIATION

For a challenge, try using smaller beads to make earrings or charms to hang from a necklace or bracelet. The photo shows a bottle of real chile-pepper hot sauce that has been covered with peyote stitch, using Delica beads. For details on how to do circular peyote stitch, see Chapter 12. Individually beaded chile peppers made with size 14 beads were then added to the bottle for embellishment.

11

CORN-STITCH EARRINGS

Corn stitch and decreasing brick stitch

Intermediate

Native to the North American continent, corn has been a major food source to indigenous people. American Indian corn comes in numerous varieties, including white, yellow, red, and blue. Corn is used ceremonially since it is considered sacred to many tribes. Real dried corn is also used for various craft projects, especially those involving a fall harvest theme.

- size 11 seed bead blend in white, yellow, red, and blue (accent with gold, silver, or copper)

- size A, B, or O beading thread

- size 10 to 12 beading needle

- ear wires

- scraps of leather, Ultrasuede, or corn husks

- scissors

- clear nail polish

- white glue

Project Notes: These earrings are made with a technique called corn stitch because the beads line up in neat little rows, strongly resembling real corn. Corn stitch, ironically, is also known as square stitch or round stitch.

The tip is finished off by using decreasing brick stitch, also called Apache weave or Comanche weave, to make a small point at the end. Some beaders use real corn husks at the top of the beaded corn but this pattern uses leather strips, since they last longer. Corn husks and leather are biodegradable materials. The beaded corns can be made into earrings or hung as pendants on a necklace. They can also be made into tie tacks, lapel pins, and hair ornaments.

I. Begin by stringing 11 to 15 beads on your thread and a stop bead. The stop bead will help you orient your work since it is held in the down position, as shown. The number of beads determines the finished length of the earrings. Fifteen beads would be about 1 inch long.

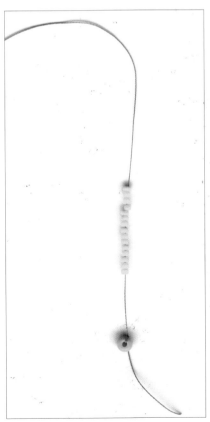

2. To begin the second row, string one bead on your needle and pass it through the last bead of the first row.

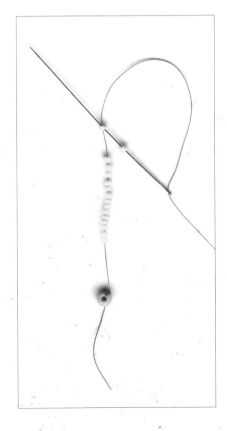

3. Pass your needle down the bead you just added.

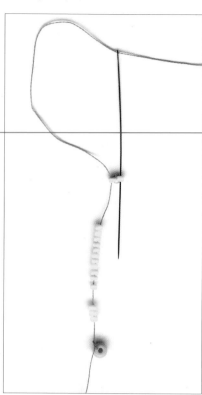

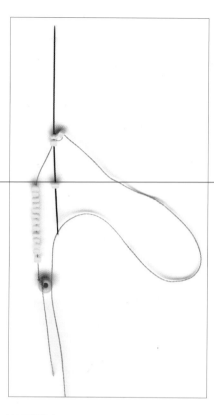

4. Pick up another bead on your needle and pass it up the second to last bead of the first row and down the bead you just added.

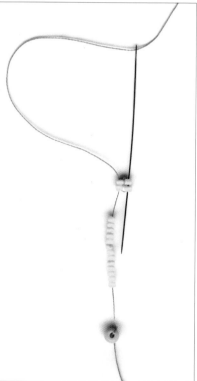

5. Continue adding beads in the same manner until you reach the end of the row. (Pick up one bead, slide one bead from the original row, and pass your needle up two beads and then down two beads.) Complete the rest of the rows, turning your work at the end of each row. Finish 7 to 9 rows to make a solid rectangle of beadwork.

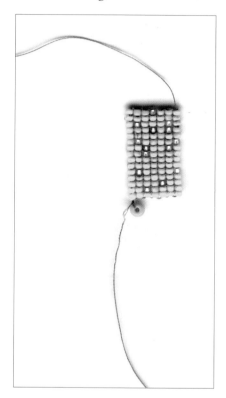

6. Wrap the beadwork around trimmed leather scraps, and sew the seam together with the same stitch without adding beads. Use a dot of white glue to hold your leather in place while you stitch it together.

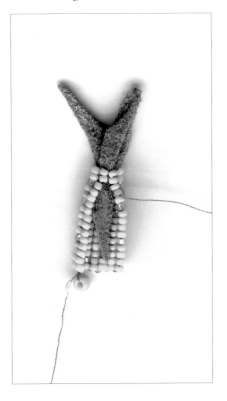

7. Finish your corn-on-the-cob by adding two rows of decreasing brick stitch (also called Apache weave and Comanche weave) on the end to bring it to a point. To decrease, string 2 beads, skip the first thread bridge and go under the second thread bridge. Complete the stitch by passing your needle back up the bead you just added. See details in Chapter 9 on how to do the "up-down-up thing."

Brick stitch or Apache weave starts off each row with two beads and continues with one bead after that.

8. Complete the stitch by passing your needle back up the bead you just added. If you have 7 rows in your corn, decrease to 5 beads and then 3 to form a point on the corn.

9. Weave your thread to the top of the corn. Make a loop of 6 to 8 beads and string the ear wire in the middle. Attach it to the other side of the corn, the third bead over. Reinforce by passing your needle and thread through the loop at least twice. Tie a half-hitch or in-line knot and weave the tail of your thread through the beadwork. Use a dot of clear nail polish to secure the knot.

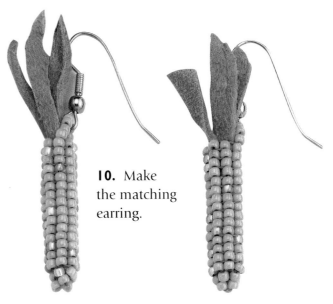

10. Make the matching earring.

VARIATIONS

Here are examples of corn in several different colors. Use them with the beaded baskets in Chapter 14 and 15 to make delightful miniatures for gifts or decoration.

12

PHOENIX KEY RING

The phoenix, a legendary winged creature, was born from the first rose in the Garden of Paradise. Many phoenix stories, with striking similarities, have been circulated by cultures all over the world. According to legend, each century the phoenix is consumed in fire and from the ashes a new phoenix rises or the old is reborn. This amazing creature is said to reside in the city of fire or the city of the sun, which, no doubt, means Phoenix, Arizona.

In a delightful story by Hans Christian Andersen, the rightful name given to the phoenix in Paradise, is poetry. The symbol of the phoenix is common among many Native Americans as well as other Southwest residents. This particular pattern came from a piece of Navajo beadwork, but the original source is unknown. Many artists consider the phoenix to be a waterfowl, such as a heron or holy swan, but classic literature refers to him as a peacock or an eagle. Regardless, the phoenix is a delightful symbol representing immortality, resurrection, and life after death. Native American beliefs usually include many concepts relating to the spirit world, sacred winged creatures, and the sun.

The huge metropolis of Phoenix, Arizona, is home to many thousands of urban American Indians who relocated to the city. Due to the migration of native people from throughout the country and intermarriages between tribes, the larger cities have an interesting blend of intertribal cultures.

In addition, native people from the entire continent, especially from Mexico and Canada, have been migrating to the United States. Many native peoples do not recognize international borders. A few of the many tribes originating from Mexico and farther south are the Huichol, Tarahumara, Seri, Mayo, Apache, Aztec, and Yaqui.

Local Arizona tribes include Apache, Chemehuevi, Cocopah, Hualapai, Havasupai, Hopi, Kaibab-Paiute, Maricopa, Mohave, Navajo, Pima, Quechan, Tohono O'odham, Yaqui, and Yavapai. To confuse matters, many tribes identify with a name different than the name recognized by the U.S. government. Examples are the Diné who are called Navajo and Yoeme who are called Yaqui. Keep in mind that Native American tribes have separate and distinct bands, histories, cultures, languages, and traditions. Historically, different tribes were often consolidated on the same reservation, so the legal distinction does not necessarily even define the cultural group.

- wooden dowel (2 inches long and ½-inch diameter)

- 2 eye screws

- leather to cover the dowel

- 2 pieces of leather lace for fringe, each about 12 inches long

- 1-inch diameter key ring

- size 11 seed beads in blue, black, maroon, red, orange, yellow-orange, yellow, and white

- 12 crow beads in complementary colors

- size 10 beading needle

- size O or B beading thread

- white glue or leather glue

- clear nail polish

Project Notes: The project itself, a beaded key ring, is a modern vestige of a (horse) riding crop. Often made of leather and horsehair, this particular key ring is beaded onto a wooden dowel, with metal hardware and leather fringe. The beads are attached with a technique called round or circular peyote stitch.

There are many variations of peyote stitch used to cover three-dimensional objects. This project teaches even-count peyote. There is also an odd-count peyote stitch which spirals continuously instead of adding a row at a time. There is also two-drop peyote stitch, three-drop peyote stitch and flat peyote stitch. Some people also refer to it as gourd stitch but there are subtle differences between the different techniques.

In earlier centuries, when horses were the primary means of transportation, the riding crop was used to motivate or communicate with a horse. Elaborate beadwork was done on such instruments for show, another example of functional art. Important symbols and designs were often woven into the beadwork to remind the owner of loftier spiritual considerations.

Since few people in modern times rely on horses for transportation, we use our beaded key rings to help us motivate and navigate our automobiles. It is a fine example of a mundane functional tool used for artistic expression and symbolism.

1. Begin by covering the pre-cut wooden dowel with fabric, like thin leather, felt, or Ultrasuede. A local hardware store will have pre-cut and pre-drilled dowels. If you cannot obtain the exact dimensions, the pattern can be easily altered to accommodate the dowel's size. Glue it in place, being careful not to overlap the seams. Stitch the seams together, if necessary. The fabric helps cushion the glass beads to prevent them from breaking with daily use.

2. Screw in the eye screws on both ends of the dowel. You're now ready to begin beading.

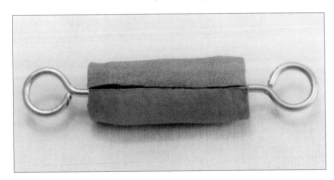

3. String 34 background color beads onto your needle and thread. Tie them in a circle around the dowel and secure with a square knot and glue with a dot of clear nail polish.

If 34 beads don't fit in a snug circle with no large gaps, the pattern can be easily adapted as long as you increase by an even number of beads. For example, 36 or 38 beads can be used to form a ring of beads. When you begin a beadwork project like this with background color beads of your choice, it is easy to fill in the extra background area needed without altering the actual pattern at all. This is a three-dimensional project, so advanced beaders are usually familiar with the technique of modifying the pattern to fit exactly. If you use smaller beads, like Delicas or cylinder beads, you'll need more beads or a smaller dowel.

4. Before you begin beading, pass your needle through one bead to conceal the knot. Pick up 1 bead, skip a bead, and pass your needle through the next bead.

5. Continue adding 1 bead every other bead. When you add the last bead of the row, your needle will pass through the same bead where your row started.

6. The next step is called the step down, where you pass your needle through the first bead you added to bring you down to the next row. You do the step down at the beginning of every row when you are doing even-count peyote stitch.

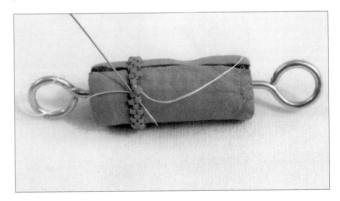

7. Continue the next row by adding one bead every other bead, following the pattern shown. By adding a bead every other bead, you are actually only completing half a row at a time.

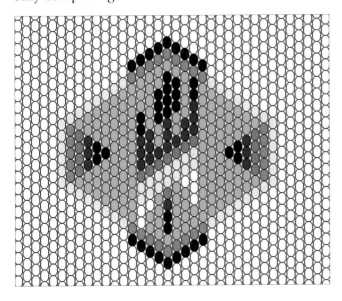

8. When you have completed the beadwork, string the leather laces through the bottom eye screw. Use a little white glue to hold the laces in place while you bead around them.

9. Tie a circle of 12 beads around the leather lace. Do five rows of peyote stitch around the leather lace. Finish by knotting, gluing, and trimming your thread. Use firm tension so that the beaded tube does not slip off.

10. Embellish the leather with crow beads. Attach the key ring to the beaded dowel.

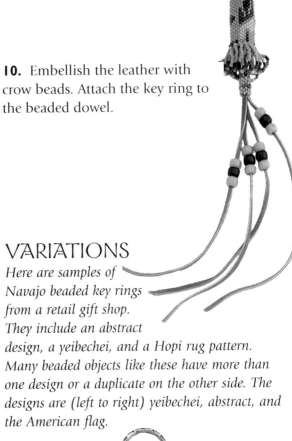

VARIATIONS

Here are samples of Navajo beaded key rings from a retail gift shop. They include an abstract design, a yeibechei, and a Hopi rug pattern. Many beaded objects like these have more than one design or a duplicate on the other side. The designs are (left to right) yeibechei, abstract, and the American flag.

13

KOKOPELLI AMULET BAG

Circular peyote stitch and flat peyote stitch

Advanced

Kokopelli is alive and well in Indian country! This Southwestern icon is an extremely popular cultural artifact, historically as well as in contemporary artwork. Many tales follow this folk character, mostly known by his physical features, a hunched back and feathers on his head.

Kokopelli symbolizes fertility. A healthy human or plant gene pool must be interspersed with "fresh genes" periodically. Interbreeding that's too close results in genetic mutations and unhealthy offspring. Some stories say that Kokopelli was happy to share his own seed, as well as plant seeds, with neighboring pueblos. Either way, his involvement among different tribal communities assured a successful crop of new life, which was good for the continuing survival of the species.

As the story goes, Kokopelli was a trader who traveled among the various pueblos or villages, trading seeds, news, music, and goods like beads. The hump on his back suggests a backpack. Many people speculate that he announced his friendly intentions by playing flute music upon his arrival to a new community. The flute is also used for teaching songs and prayers in ceremonies.

Although Kokopelli has remarkable commercial appeal, most consumers never look past his obvious physical characteristics. He represents much more than his cartoonlike image would suggest.

Symbolically, the artist can take liberties with interpretations to tell his or her own story. A modern version of a medicine bag, this beaded bag holds objects and fetishes that remind the wearer of the spiritual nature of his existence. The medicine bag can also hold healing herbs and plants that correct physical ailments as well as promoting good health. It is also a medium for storytelling through images and designs.

In my example, Kokopelli is a holy man traveling from the desert floor to higher mountain elevations. He carries the sacred pipe used ceremonially to promote spiritual teachings among native peoples. The smoke is an ethereal representation of prayers sent to a higher spiritual plane. Musical notes coming from a flute also represent prayers since sounds are not readily detectable in the visual realm.

Another prominent image is the saguaro cactus. The Tohono O'odham people of the desert Southwest believe that the giant saguaro cacti literally house their ancestors. As such, they are treated with great respect and reverence. The saguaro cactus is an incredible form of plant life that adapts well to the harsh desert climate, similar to the climatic adaptations the native people of the Southwest have made.

The eagle feathers are sacred among native people since the eagle possesses many profound characteristics renowned in the animal kingdom. They literally exist on a higher plane and have keen vision, here used metaphorically to encourage people to transcend their cognition to a higher level.

The turquoise, bone, and coral beads used in the fringe represent rock life, animal life, and sea life, that all need to exist in harmony in the natural world.

The actual colors of the beads used can symbolize many things. The color blue is used to represent water, which replenishes the land and is a necessity for survival. White represents the spiritual death that's essential to achieving a spiritual transcendence. The sunset colors of red, orange, and yellow merely mimic some of the prominent colors of the desert architecture.

We encourage bead artists to tell their own stories and identify their own symbolism of what is sacred and holy. Although we include a bead pattern, you may want to alter the pattern to personalize your own amulet or medicine bag with your own colors, fetishes, design elements, and fringe.

- empty cardboard tube from a toilet paper roll

- size 10 beading needle

- size A, B, or O beading thread

- 2 tubes of background color beads (We used Delica #203 pearl cream.)

- 1 tube each of Delica beads used in the pattern: yellow # 53, orange # 45, red # 603, purple #661, turquoise # 238, blue # 47, gray #52, coral #175, green #797, green # 133, bronze #322, brown # 769

- assorted embellishment beads, gem chips, and charms

- measuring tape

- scissors

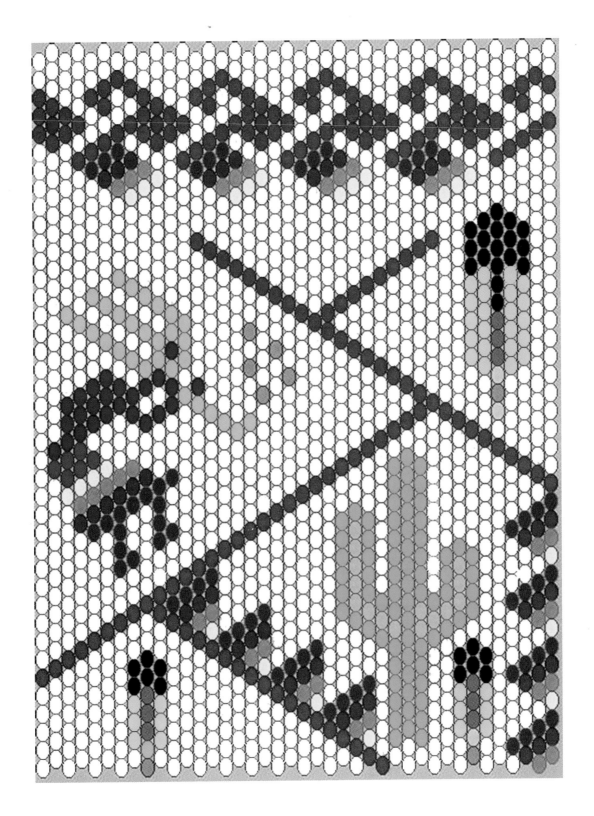

Project Notes: This Kokopelli amulet bag uses a round or circular peyote stitch. Since the pattern uses an even number of beads, it is called "even count." The amulet bag is beaded around a recycled tube from the center of a roll of toilet paper. The bottom of the bag is made with a technique called flat peyote stitch that gives the bag depth.

The directions here are for the bag only; an advanced beader usually knows how to add fringe and necklace straps. Without fringe, the finished bag is about 2 × 3 inches.

The graph pattern, which is exactly 40 beads across, is for the front only. The pattern can be duplicated on the back or another pattern may be used to make it reversible. The bead count from the top to bottom is 42 beads. You have the option of making the back of the bag a solid color, which makes the beading go faster.

1. Cut the cardboard tube lengthwise to customize the fit. Use transparent tape or masking tape to alter the size to fit the number of beads used.

2. String exactly 80 beads on your thread and slide them to the bottom of the thread, leaving a 6-inch tail. All the beads will be background color beads. Tie your beads into a loose ring around the cardboard and tape the cardboard in place. There should be a small gap of at least one bead wide in your thread before you tie a square knot. This helps your beadwork to have a fluid texture instead of being stiff and rigid. Tape your tail to the cardboard so that it will be out of the way while you are beading.

3. Following the pattern, you will be adding one bead every other bead, all the way around the ring. To add a bead, you pick up a bead, skip a bead and pass your needle through the next bead. The beads will stack up in the pattern shown.

4. When you reach the end of the first row, you will "drop down" by passing your needle through the first bead you added from the previous row. This is repeated at the end of every row.

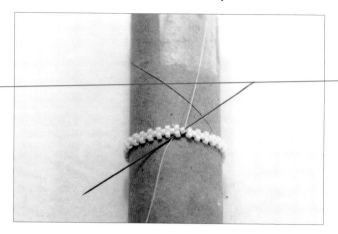

5. Carefully follow the pattern graph to bead the body of the amulet bag.

6. To finish the bottom, continue weaving 40 beads across either the back of the bag for three rows in flat peyote stitch. Remember that each row is actually only half a row in peyote stitch, so you will be going back and forth six times. When you reach the end of the first row, you change directions and weave the opposite direction. If this is unclear, refer to Chapter 4 on flat peyote stitch, which is a two-dimensional rather than a three-dimensional beading technique. These few rows make up the bottom of the bag. The photo shows where your needle should exit from the back of the bag.

7. You will be changing directions at the end of each row. Like round peyote stitch, you will be adding one bead every other bead.

8. When you are finished, the few rows form a flap at the bottom of the bag, which is turned under and attached to the opposite side of the bag.

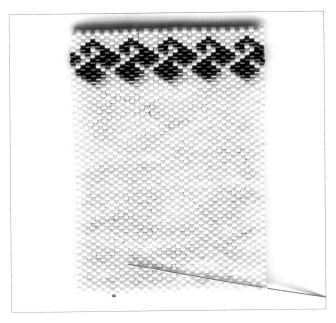

11. The bottom of the bag should appear smooth and seamless.

12. To complete the project, all you need to do is add fringe and a necklace strap to your amulet bag.

9. The two pieces should align just like a zipper, and this is frequently called a zipper stitch.

10. Without adding any beads, run your needle through the beads that stick out from front to back until your bag is all zipped up.

14

NETTED BASKET

Basket weaving has been an art form for millennia. Various natural materials woven together serve a very functional purpose of carrying and storing items. Today, baskets are often used for decoration. Native Americans and other cultures continue to make many different types and shapes of baskets; collectors actively seek unique and lovely ones. Pima and Papago (Tohono O'odham) basket weavers hold a strong reputation for being the most technically proficient basket weavers among the Native American tribes. However, the Hopi, Tarahumara, and Apache basket weavers also hold an excellent reputation for making specific types of beautiful baskets. Many different tribal members throughout Indian country have awesome skills and styles in basket weaving; some of their works are included in guilds and museum exhibitions.

Similar to pottery, each artist has his or her own unique way of creating signature art. A Tohono O'odham woman taught me the basic rules of basket construction, which I translated into beadwork. Since these baskets are made of glass beads, weight becomes a factor if they are very big. These beaded baskets make adorable miniatures and are quite functional for holding your little harvest of beaded chile peppers and beaded corns. (See Chapters 10 and 11 to learn how to make those projects.)

- 3 tubes of size 11 beads

- size 10 beading needle

- size B or O beading thread

- clear nail polish, satin or matte coating, or fabric stiffener that dries clear

Project Notes: This beaded basket was made with size 11 seed beads. However, you can make it with smaller beads for more pattern detail. This particular project pattern uses a different color in each row to make it easier to see which row you are currently working on. Once you learn the basic circular netting stitch, also called Huichol lace, you can experiment with the pattern of colors and the number of beads used to sculpt the basket to the shape you want. It takes a little practice, so be patient with your efforts. Since this is a three-dimensional project, you have to think out of the box. It helps to study different basket shapes and styles.

Although the materials are different from those used to weave baskets, the rules of construction are similar. Keep these three basic rules in mind: (1) Increasing the number of beads will help your walls flare out. (2) When you stop increas-

ing, the walls will start to go up. (3) When you decrease, your walls will turn inward.

1. Begin with a ring of 12 beads. Tie them in a circle and use clear nail polish to glue your knot. Pass the needle through one bead to conceal your knot. Wait until it dries before trimming.

2. Add 3 beads every other bead, which will give 6 points to your second row.

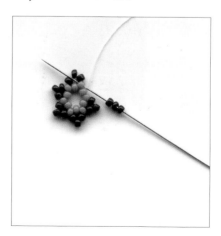

3. To begin your third row, move your needle to the peak bead by passing it through 2 beads. (The peak bead is the middle one.) Add 5 beads from peak to peak all the way around the ring. At the end of each row, tie a half-hitch knot and pass your needle to the peak bead.

4. From this point, add 7 beads from peak to peak, all the way around the circle. Tie a half-hitch or in-line knot at the end of each row to keep your tension. Move your needle to the peak bead before you begin your next row.

5. Row 5 is different. Add 5 beads, from the second to the sixth bead. Then add 5 beads from the sixth to the second bead all the way around to the end of the row.

6. For row 6, add 5 beads from peak to peak.

7. For row 7, add 5 beads from peak to peak.

8. For row 8, add 1 "point" between each section of 5 beads from the previous row. The point bead is added between sections. This helps you build walls. Copper beads are used in this step so that you can clearly see what we call a "point bead." (See photo.)

9. For row 9, from the point bead, add 3 beads and pass your needle through the next peak bead. Continue adding 3 beads from peak to point and point to peak.

10. For row 10, add 3 beads from peak to peak. Repeat for several rows until your walls begin to curve upward. From this point on, keep adding rows until your basket takes on the appropriate shape.

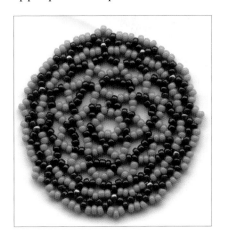

11. Use your thread tension to control the shape of your basket. It usually takes about 3 rows before you start to see the shape change. Keep building your wall until it reaches a good depth.

The 5-bead finishing row shown makes a lip that flares out, if you like that effect on your basket. Use distilled water to shape your basket and let it dry. If you choose, you can use clear nail polish to stiffen your basket to hold its final shape. You could also use satin or matte-finish craft coating or fabric stiffeners as long as they dry clear.

VARIATIONS

In the photo are several examples of baskets made with different patterns and different sizes of beads. Laura Moreno made the basket on the far left with Delica beads. The basket at the top was made with size 14 beads, and the one on the right with size 13 beads. The bottom was made with size 11 beads.

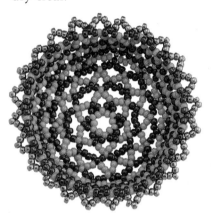

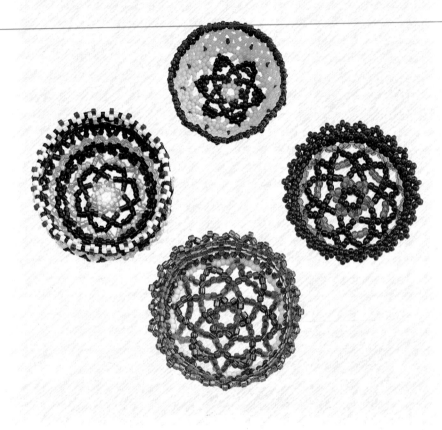

15

FLAT ROUND PEYOTE BASKET

Flat round peyote stitch

Advanced

This is a different type of beaded basket with a much tighter weave than the netted basket in Chapter 14. It tends to hold its shape better with little or no stiffening with clear nail polish. The baskets shown are more similar to shallow baskets or trays rather than deep baskets for carrying heavy loads, like the famous Apache burden baskets used to collect the harvest. Basket making traditionally required a great deal of work, including the gathering of raw materials. Weavers could spend a lot of extra time and effort to dye materials to get certain colors for their weaving patterns. Making baskets out of beads is much easier on your hands and eliminates the gathering and dying steps of basket weaving.

Since this is a three-dimensional object, it can also be used as a jewelry component for making necklace pendants, pins, brooches, or hair decorations. They also make darling miniatures for use in decorating or actual functional baskets for small treasures, like rings or earrings. This project is an exercise in basket appreciation because of the sculpting involved to make a nice shape. Keep in mind that it takes a little practice to obtain a nice shape.

- 1 tube each of four different colors of size 11 beads

- size 10 beading needle

- size O or B beading thread

- clear nail polish

Project Notes: It takes time to master the thread tension and stitch, but the actual flat round peyote basket is quite small, measuring only about 1½ inches in diameter. With some practice, you'll find it easier to control the tension and to form a nice, smooth shape. If you want a flat object, keep your tension relaxed and keep increasing every third row. If you stop increasing, the sides of your basket will start to form. If you decrease, the sides will start to curve in. In this particular project pattern, the 2-bead black spokes are the increases. Follow the illustrations closely to learn the stitch before you experiment with a complicated pattern.

1. Tie 6 beads in a ring. Secure with a knot and glue with clear nail polish.

2. Add 1 bead between every bead.

3. Increase by adding 2 beads between every pop-up bead.

4. Add a bead between every pop-up bead and between increase beads. The increase beads shown are black.

5. Add a bead between every pop-up bead.

6. Increase by adding 2 beads on top of the previous increase two rows back. Study the pictures to see how the pattern develops.

7. Repeat instructions 4, 5, and 6. If you want a flat object, keep your tension relaxed and keep increasing every third row. If you stop increasing, the sides of the basket will start to form. If you decrease, the sides will start to curve in.

8. Keep in mind that you need to use your thread tension to sculpt the beadwork into a nice shape. See the picture of the finished basket below to try out an interesting edging for your basket.

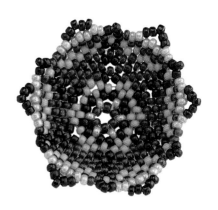

VARIATIONS

Many variations are possible when you experiment with different colors, sizes of beads, and patterns. The baskets can be made with Czech beads, which tend to be oval, and Japanese beads, which tend to be square. They look nice when made with cylinder beads and smaller sizes like 13, 14, and 15. The photo below shows many interesting basket patterns. Most of the smallest baskets were made by Gale Manning, who specializes in miniatures.

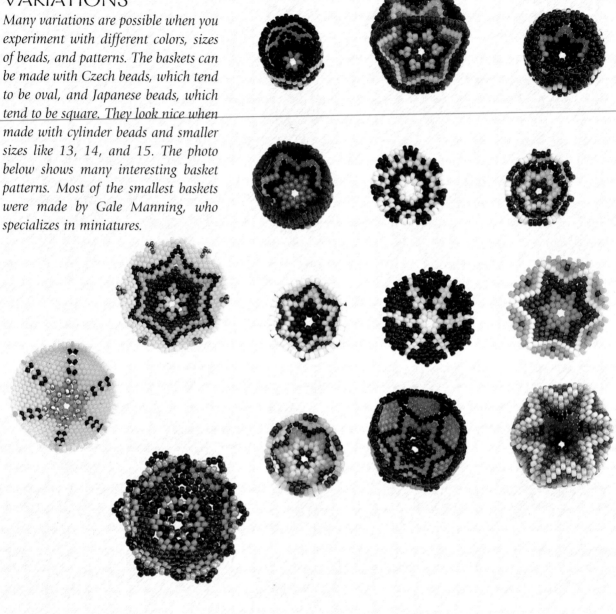

16

POWWOW PERFUME BAG

Circular horizontal netting

Advanced

This project uses a versatile horizontal netting technique for making a mini-bag for many functions or social activities. A strap is attached so that you can carry it around your neck or hang it for a decoration. You will learn how to increase the width or length of the bag to customize it to fit many different shapes. This bag can be used for carrying a perfume atomizer or scented oil, as well as lip gloss, medications such as nitroglycerin tablets, inhalers, or eye drops; or use it for contact lenses, money, credit cards, or other necessities or valuables. You can also hang it from your car's rear view mirror or hang it in your bath or nursery with a selected air freshener.

On the powwow circuit, these mini-bags are also called possible bags, anything bags, or amulet bags. The Powwow Perfume Bag is a good example of functional art since it has a very practical use in addition to personal adornment. Whether you are a participant or a spectator, you can proudly wear your own beaded bag to your next powwow.

- l large plastic bead tube to bead around (can substitute with a wider tubular object)

- several complementary colors of size 11 seed beads (minimum of 2)

- size A, B, or O beading thread

- size 10 beading needle

- fetishes and embellishment beads for fringe and strap

Project Notes: This bag is relatively small so that you will not be carrying excessive weight around your neck. The finished bag measures about 2 to 4 inches long, prior to attaching the necklace strap and not including the fringe. The bag pictured uses size 11 seed beads, but larger or smaller beads can be used for a different effect. The circular netting results in a sturdy but fluid beadwork fabric capable of adapting to many three-dimensional shapes. The bag in the photo is embellished with amethyst tube beads, garnets, jade, pearls, fire-polish beads, and Bali silver spacers. It is great fun to use assorted special beads or one-of-a-kind gems.

1. Begin by stringing 3 main-color beads and 1 marker bead. This pattern comprises a set of 4 beads. Repeat until you have 8 sets of beads. Tie in a circle around the plastic bead tube using a square knot. Make sure that your needle is exiting the marker bead. If you need to make your perfume bag smaller or larger, increase or decrease in sets of 4 beads. Use a dot of clear nail polish to secure the knot.

2. Add 5 main-color beads, from marker to marker, all the way around the ring. Since you are working in a circle, your last addition of 5 beads goes into the same bead as the beginning bead of the initial ring. Tie a half-hitch knot at the end of each row.

3. To begin your next row, you have to "drop down" by running your needle to the center or peak bead (third bead) of the five beads added to the last row.

4. For the next row, you will be adding 3 beads from peak to peak.

5. Continue the pattern of adding a row of 5 beads (from peak to peak) and then add a row of 3 beads (from peak to peak) until your bag is long enough to accommodate the perfume bottle, about 2 to 4 inches. End with a row of three beads.

6. To start the bottom of the bag, you will be decreasing by adding 3 beads from peak to peak. On the next row, add 1 bead from peak to peak. On the last row, add 1 bead from peak to peak. You may need to adjust the bead count slightly to make it fit neatly.

7. Tie a secure knot and seal with a dot of clear nail polish. Leave your bag plain or add fringe and embellishment. You can also bead a flap with flat peyote stitch. (See Chapter 4 for details.)

8. Finish your bag by stringing beads to form a necklace strap and adding fringe.

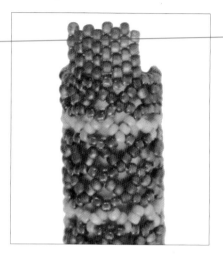

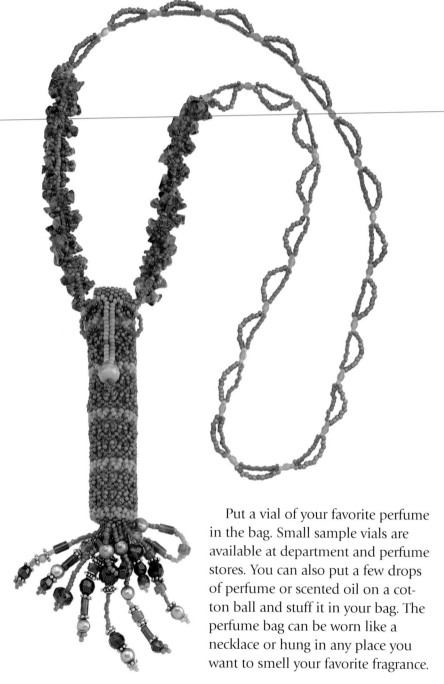

Put a vial of your favorite perfume in the bag. Small sample vials are available at department and perfume stores. You can also put a few drops of perfume or scented oil on a cotton ball and stuff it in your bag. The perfume bag can be worn like a necklace or hung in any place you want to smell your favorite fragrance.

VARIATIONS

For a challenge, try introducing more colors to experiment with patterns and designs. Use different sizes of objects to bead around, like a medicine bottle or perfume bottle. Remove the bottle after beading around it to create a fluid or pliable bag shape. You can also cut a plastic bead tube with scissors to get a perfect fit for your bag frame if you prefer a more stable shape. Below is a photo of two perfume bags; Terri LaBrosse beaded the bag on the right and Laura Moreno the bag on the left. The choice of colors and embellishment fetishes show creative alternatives.

17

NAVAJO BEAD RUG

Loom weaving

Intermediate

For centuries, the Navajo and Pueblo Indians of the Southwest have been perfecting their weaving skills, beginning with domestic grasses and cotton. Under the influence of Spanish explorers in the 16th century, sheep and sheep herding came to the people. The transition to weaving wool was not difficult for accomplished weavers. The Navajo style, pattern, quality, and designs of beautiful rugs and blankets have a worldwide reputation.

This beaded rug is a replica of only one of many designs recognized as a Navajo design. The particular pattern shown is an adaptation of one from a loomed necklace made by Louise Harmon from Kayenta, Arizona. The duplication of the design in a different art form serves as a tribute to the history of the art of weaving. Bead weaving is distinctly different from basket weaving and rug weaving. Contemporary artists are using nontraditional media and materials to incorporate into their artwork.

The craft of weaving generally results in functional items, such as baskets and blankets. A good blanket keeps cold and moisture away from the wearer's skin. A good basket is able to carry a burden, store food, or hold water. The art of weaving involves intricate use of colors, patterns, and designs. Facets of history, culture, language, and tradition have been woven into rugs. However, our beaded rug project is entirely useless, except as an object of beauty. Societies enjoying the luxuries of abundant resources and time can create something with no obvious function apart from its aesthetic appeal.

- size O thread (Use heavier thread for larger beads.)

- size 14 seed beads in red, white, gray, black, and bronze or gold

- leather or Ultrasuede scraps for backing

- size 12 beading needle

- bead loom

- sharp scissors or leather shears

- clear nail polish or thin white glue

Project Notes: A bead loom is required for this project. The one pictured right was bought in a retail American Indian arts store. The pattern included was made with size 14 Japanese beads and measures 1⅞ × 1⅝ inches, not including the leather backing. Larger beads can be used, but they will change the beaded rug's dimensions. Try to choose beads that are fairly uniform in size. Any type of backing, such as leather or Ultrasuede, can be used and cut to make fringe.

1. Tie a knot around the screw head on the loom to secure your thread. String the thread from front to back, wrapping the thread around the screw head on the other side of the loom. String your loom with one more thread than the number of beads across the pattern. The pattern shown has 41 beads, so you need to string 42 threads.

bead loom

2. After you've strung the loom, tie your thread securely to maintain good tension. With a square knot, tie a separate piece of thread, about 1 yard long, onto the outermost warp thread. Most right-handed people tie the thread on the left side and weave from right to left.

3. Thread your needle and pick up the bead colors required in the pattern to begin your first row. The pattern is symmetrical, so you can start at either the top or the bottom. For the first row, you will pick up 3 red beads, 35 white beads, and 3 red beads.

4. Passing the needle and thread under the warp threads, push the beads up between the threads and pass your needle through the beads from right to left. Be careful not to pierce the threads with your needle.

5. Your first row will dictate the width of the beaded piece. To secure the tension, weave behind the first row for 6 to 8 rows with thread only. This helps to maintain your tension while you are getting started. After you complete those rows, use clear nail polish on the woven threads to stiffen them. This will keep your beadwork stable when you eventually take your beadwork off the loom.

6. Continue following the pattern until you are finished with the bead weaving. Secure again by weaving 6 to 8 rows without beads; tie off and stiffen the thread with clear nail polish.

7. Before cutting the threads to remove the beadwork from the loom, place transparent tape on both sides of the threads, top and bottom.

8. Trim the transparent tape with sharp scissors and neatly fold under the beadwork to conceal your threads.

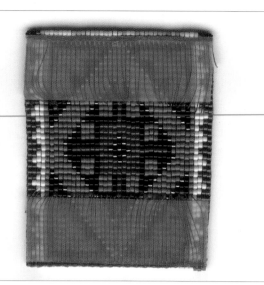

Try using your rug to display fetishes and trinkets like baskets or miniature dolls.

9. Mount the miniature rug onto a piece of leather or Ultrasuede that's longer than the piece of beadwork. Stitch along the edge of the beadwork to secure it onto the backing. Use colored thread and small stitches to conceal the stitching on the edges. Use sharp scissors to cut fringe.

18

KOKOPELLI PIN

*Increasing and
decreasing
Apache weave,
flat peyote stitch,
and corn stitch*

Advanced

The many faces and forms of Kokopelli make this project a versatile way to show your proud membership in the Kokopelli fan club. Whether he is drawn, painted, carved, molded, or beaded, his image persists in the art world. (See Chapter 13 for historic details.) Since the image of Kokopelli has appeared in Native American cave art, many people believe that he was a real person. The Hopi Indians have a kachina, or wooden figurine, with the same name, but their kachina shows little resemblance to the popular icon.

Kachinas are used ceremonially to represent ancestral spirits and to reveal some aspect of life. The dolls are often carved out of the roots of the cottonwood tree. They are used ceremonially to teach important life lessons and symbolism to children and other tribal members. Generally, kachinas are considered benevolent. Kokopelli is considered a symbol of fertility.

- 3 complementary colors of cylinder beads (turquoise, fuchsia, and purple shown)

- black bead for the eye

- 10 transparent clear beads

- size A, B or O beading thread

- size 10 beading needle

- clear nail polish, acrylic stiffener, or matte fabric stiffener

- jewelry adhesive

Project Notes: After you complete the beadwork for the Kokopelli figure, you'll glue a pin back or tie tack to the back. You can stiffen the beadwork with clear nail polish or jewelry acrylic finish. Fabric stiffener is also an option if it doesn't affect the finish of the glass beads. Attach the beaded pin to your lapel, tie, collar tips, hat, purse, or other articles of clothing. This is a relatively quick project for the advanced beader. He measures about 2 inches tall and ½ inch wide at the waist. You may want to try out a wide variety of bead sizes and colors.

Here we've beaded the basic body with Apache weave or brick stitch, and the flute with corn stitch. Begin beading at the widest part of the body and bead up toward the head. Then weave the thread down to the starting point. Using the basic stitch, increase and decrease as the pattern dictates. Transparent crystal beads or matte translucent white beads create the space between the arms and face.

1. Starting at the widest point of the body, bead a two-bead row of flat peyote stitch for the base. For detailed instructions, see Chapter 8.

2. Following the pattern, increase and decrease as necessary to form the shape. Find detailed instructions in Chapter 9 on how to increase and decrease with this stitch.

3. Bead the flute with a square or corn stitch. See Chapter 11 for detailed instructions.

4. When you've completed the body, stiffen the beadwork with clear nail polish or artist's acrylic finish.

5. Glue a pin back or tie tack to the beadwork with strong jewelry adhesive.

19

MEDICINE WHEEL

The medicine wheel is a Native American teaching tool. Also called a sacred hoop, *the medicine wheel represents a symbol-rich spiritual philosophy that helps people understand their relation to the universe. Its abstract meaning operates on many levels. The term* medicine *implies that it has healing qualities and helps maintain or recover balance. Many Native American tribes use the medicine wheel, but the symbolism varies somewhat from tribe to tribe.*

The basic shape of the wheel is a circle, which has no beginning and no end. The circle defines a dynamic cycle and can be used to define nature's four seasons: spring, summer, fall, and winter. The circle shape is found everywhere in nature; the earth, sun, and moon are all round.

The basic symbolism of the four directions—north, east, south, and west—indicated in the four intersecting lines, helps define our place on the wheel. The cycle of life includes birth, childhood, adulthood, and death. The medicine wheel also draws on the elements of human nature defined as physical, emotional, mental, and spiritual. The four intersecting lines also define the spiritual center of the universe and our relationship to all of creation. The four sacred colors of black, white, red, and yellow suggest the human races.

This general medicine wheel description cannot be authoritative for any one tribe or individual Native American, and the wheel may embody still more layers of symbols. American Indian and non-Indian community elders, spiritual leaders, and alcohol and drug addiction counselors use it as a teaching tool. The medicine wheel is not something magical or powerful in and of itself. It requires deep understanding and exploration of all aspects of ourselves in relation to the entire universe. Like other spiritual studies and serious matters, the medicine wheel requires time devoted to exploring and pursing knowledge. This beaded medicine wheel can provide a first step toward understanding and healing.

- 1-inch diameter metal earring hoop
- silver metallic thread (available at fabric stores)
- beading needle size 10 or big-eye needle
- cylinder beads-black, white, red, yellow, brown, amber, and silver-lined copper
- jewelry cement
- turquoise chip (optional)
- split ring (for hanging) or tie tack pin (for wearing)
- leather lace, satin cord, cotton cord, or sterling-silver chain

Project Notes: This medicine-wheel pendant or ornament consists of a metal hoop that is beaded on the edge with metallic thread. The colors of the four directions are then attached so that they intersect in the center of the wheel. The beaded feathers are then made individually and attached so that they hang off the sides and bottom of the wheel. The resulting ornament can be made into a pendant with a pin attachment for decorating clothing, a purse, guitar strap, or a hat. A leather or beaded strap can be added to hang the ornament as a necklace or on a car rearview mirror.

1. To create the hoop, thread your needle with about a yard of thread and tie a square knot onto the hoop, as shown.

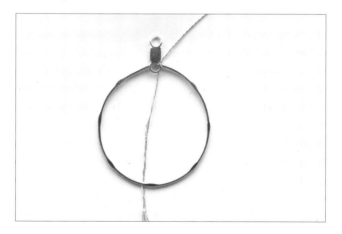

2. Glue the knot with lightweight jewelry cement and wait for it to dry before trimming the tail.

3. Pick up eight white beads on your needle and slide them down toward the hoop. The red beads are for illustration only.

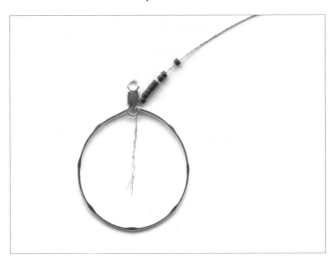

4. Pass the needle under the hoop and back through the last four beads added.

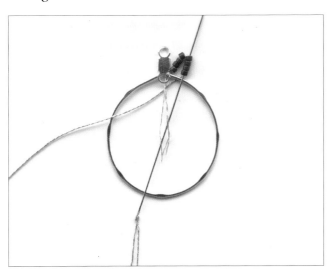

5. Tighten your thread so the beads stand up and pick up four more beads.

6. Go under the hoop and back through the four beads just added.

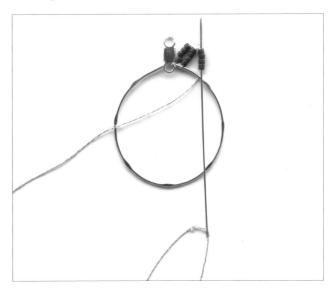

7. Continue adding beads in the same manner, all the way around the hoop. Finish off the end by weaving your thread back through the last four sections of beads and tying a knot so that it doesn't show.

8. The center cross (optional) is made by attaching your thread to the small loop at the top of the hoop and stringing beads from top to bottom. Pass your needle under the hoop and back through the beads before adding the side beads. A beaded feather can also be used to hang from the point where the lines intersect. Sterling-silver feathers and hand-carved or painted bone feathers can also be used. The small turquoise chip (optional) was glued to the center with jewelry cement.

9. Make the feathers separately by using increasing Comanche weave (also called brick stitch and Apache weave), according the pattern in Chapter 9.

10. When you are finished with one feather, use your existing thread to attach it to the medicine wheel. Attach the feather to either the hoop or the beaded edge so that it hangs nicely with the thread and knot concealed. Feathers can also be attached to the center of the hoop. Another design uses two or four feathers hanging from the bottom of the hoop.

11. To make a necklace, attach a split ring to the top ring on the hoop. Thread some leather lace, silk cord, or sterling-silver chain through the split ring to make a necklace strap or car ornament.

12. To make a hat pin or brooch, add pin-back or tie-tack hardware.

VARIATIONS

Here are samples of medicine wheels with a feather hanging inside it (left), project medicine wheel (center), and a medicine wheel with a beaded dream-catcher web in the center (right).

NATIVE AMERICAN SPIRITUALITY *cannot be easily explained or understood without thoroughly investigating the numerous facets, subtleties, and nuances of native cultures and beliefs. Active American Indian communities, who live their spiritual philosophy as a daily lifestyle through arts and cultural festivities, hold a wealth of information. For more information, check sources such as books, museums, and the Internet. Social events open to the public like powwows and American Indian art exhibitions offer the opportunity to meet native artists and beaders of many different cultures. But the best way is to get hands-on experience by trying your favorite bead projects here and, again, by letting the beads speak to you.*

LEATHER MEDICINE
BAG PATTERN

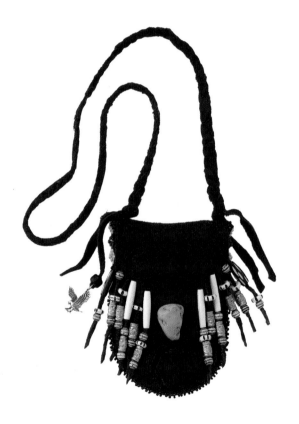

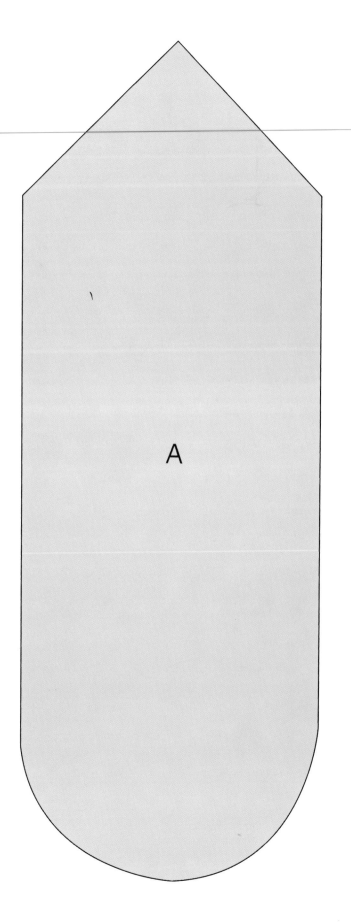

A

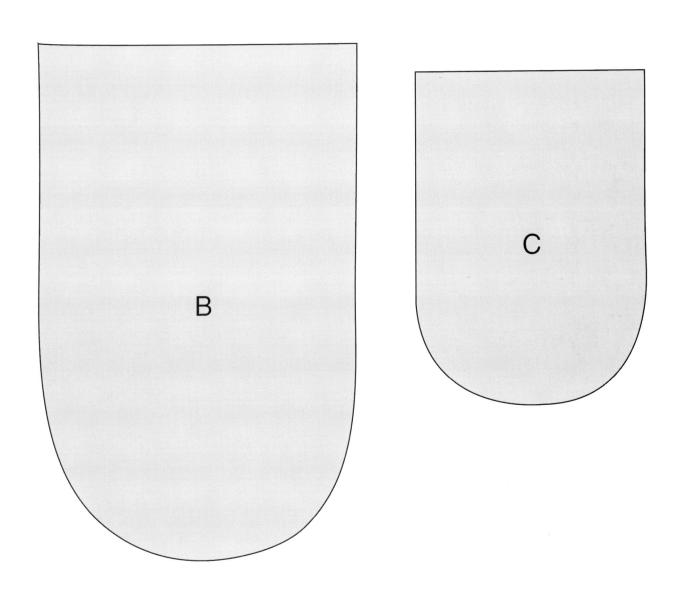

B

C

PEYOTE-STITCH GRAPH

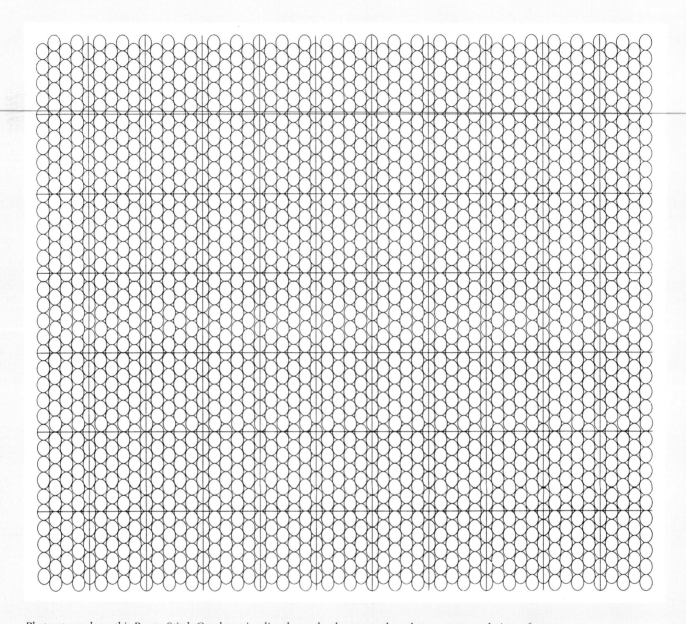

Photocopy and use this Peyote-Stitch Graph to visualize the work, plan your color scheme, or create designs of your own.

BRICK-STITCH GRAPH

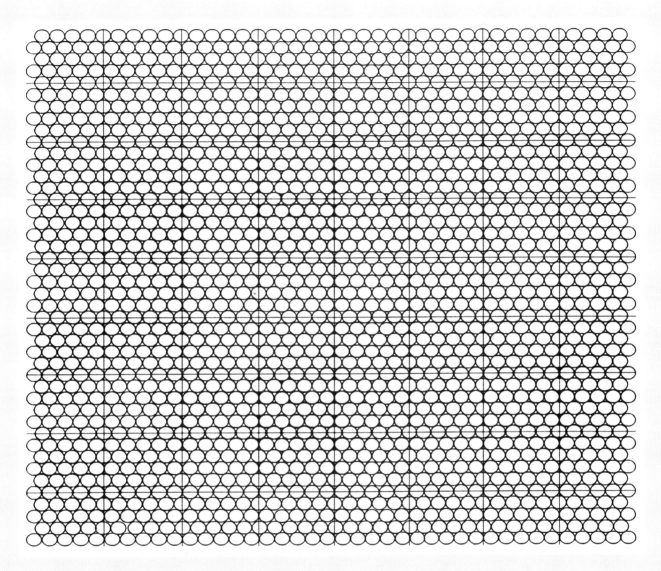

Photocopy and use this Brick-Stitch Graph to visualize the work, plan your color scheme, or create designs of your own. The brick stich is also called the Apache weave or the Comanche weave.

LOOM OR SQUARE-STITCH GRAPH

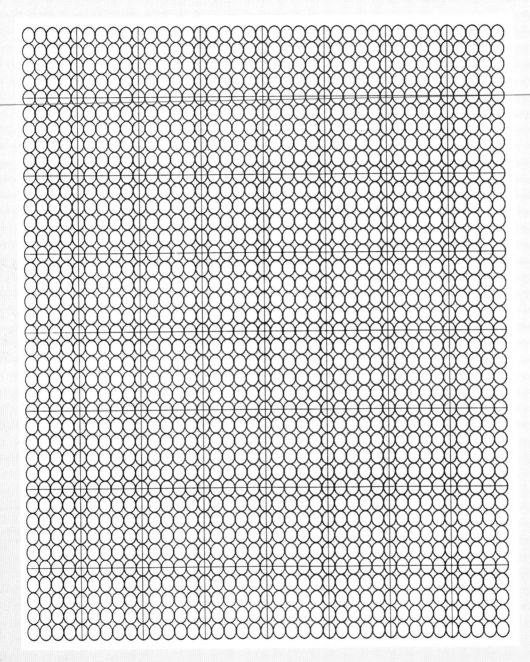

Photocopy and use this Loom or Square-Stitch Graph to visualize the work, plan your color scheme, or create designs of your own.

BEADWORK GLOSSARY

abalone

a type of shell that is polished, drilled, and used as a bead or button. It is highly prized by beaders and jewelry makers because of its lustrous finish that's similar to the natural coating found on pearls.

Apache weave

a beading technique also called Comanche weave and brick stitch. It is frequently used to make earrings with a triangular top since the stitch automatically decreases by one bead every row.

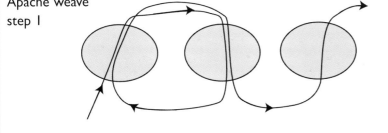

Apache weave
step 1

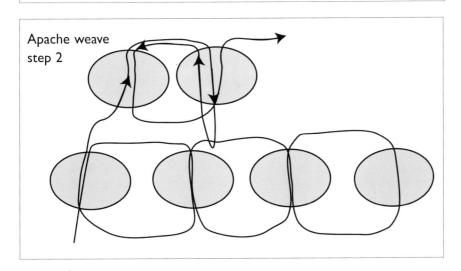

Apache weave
step 2

appliquè

a beading technique, also called couching, in which beads are tacked down onto fabric or leather with a needle and thread.

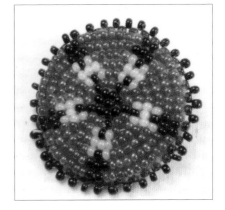

artificial sinew

a stringing material made of waxed polypropylene.

aurora borealis

a rainbow finish applied to beads.

bead finishes

color or coating applied to the outside of beads. Many combinations or finishes, such as transparent frosted aurora borealis or silver-lined matte, are available. Glass beads may also have opaque, transparent, ceylon, frosted, iridescent, metallic, luster, luminous, satin, and inside color(s).

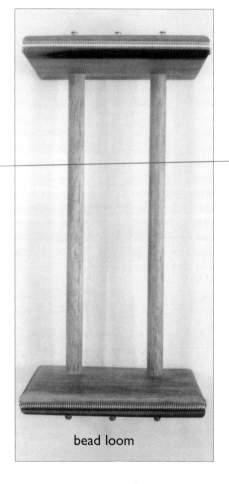

bead loom

14, and 15. The smaller the size, the larger the bead. Conversely, the larger the size, the smaller the bead. (For instance, a size 15 is smaller than a size 14 bead, and a size 8 bead is bigger than a 10, 11, 12, and so on.)

bead thread

a special thread designed for weaving and stringing beads, usually made of a sturdy synthetic, like nylon or polyester, rather than a biodegradable natural fiber, like cotton. It comes in a variety of colors and sizes, including A, O, B, D, and F. The size of thread required for a particular project depends on the size of the bead hole and the weight of the project. Bead thread is also available waxed to improve the tension of the stitch. You can buy thread conditioners that minimize tangles and knots. Bead thread is sold in bobbins, spools, and on cards.

bead types

seed beads are made from glass rods or canes cut to make individual beads. They are then heated to make smooth oval shapes, although some are more squared. The main bead manufacturers are in Japan, Czech Republic, Italy, and France.

beads with luster finish

Unique bead types are created by adding a variety of finishes, shapes, and facets. Examples include Charlottes, bugles, three-cuts, Delicas, hex beads, and white hearts.

bead wire

a wire cable that is coated with nylon. It comes in a variety of diameters or gauges. The size of wire required for a particular project depends on the size of the bead hole and the weight of the project.

bead loom

a wooden, plastic, or metal structure designed specifically for bead weaving. Looms are sold commercially, but you can easily construct one at home. Bead looms are useful for making large pieces of beadwork, such as belts, hatbands, or bead strips for embellishing fabric or leather.

bead sizes

commonly manufactured seed bead sizes are 8, 10, 11, 12, 13,

beading needle

a specially designed needle for doing beadwork. The appropriate size to choose for a project depends on the size of bead holes and whether the stitch requires more than one pass of thread.

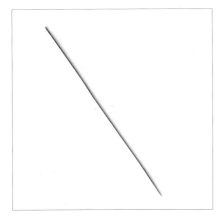

big-eye needle

a special beading needle that separates in the middle to form a needle with a large eye for easier threading.

bone-hair pipe

a tubular bead made of bone or shell, also called bone hairpipe. It is often seen in museum

pieces of chokers and breast-plates. While once considered a type of battle armor, it is now commonly seen in chokers and dance regalia.

brick stitch

a beading technique also called Apache weave and Comanche weave. Although the flat, two-dimensional form of the stitch is most common, it can also be done in a circular, three-dimensional form. Also see the Brick-Stitch Graph on p. 109.

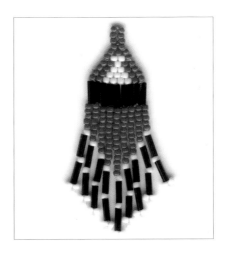

bugle beads

tubular-shaped glass beads that area a very popular shape for

jewelry design. They come in 1 mm, 2mm, 3mm, and 5mm sizes most commonly and are available in a variety of colors and finishes. The beads pictured are twisted bugles with a matte finish.

cabochon

a highly polished and cut gem-stone that is flat on one side for use as a jewelry component. Cabochons are often used with a precious-metal bezel or a beaded bezel.

cedar seeds

seeds from a cedar tree that are drilled for use as beads. They are also called ghost beads because of their reported use during the historic Ghost Dance, which was once forbidden. The essential oil from the

cedar tree that gives off its characteristic smell has medicinal antibiotic properties. Often referred to as Grandfather Cedar, the leaf is used in cleansing ceremonies.

ceylon beads
a pearlized finish on beads that tend to be in pastel colors.

chile stitch
a three-dimensional bead stitch, also called log cabin, alligator, or gecko stitch. The specific origin of the stitch is uncertain, but many South American trinkets for tourists on the market use this stitch. The chile (or chili) stitch refers to the chile pepper.

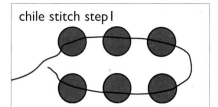

chile stitch step1

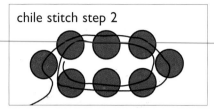

chile stitch step 2

circular Comanche weave
a beading stitch used for making round flat objects, such as a necklace pendant.

circular netting
a three-dimensional beading technique used to cover objects.

clasp
hardware or finding used to close a necklace or bracelet.

Comanche weave
a beading technique also called Apache weave or brick stitch.

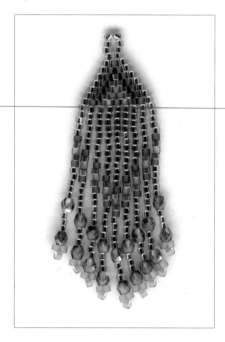

concho
a concave silver disk with a button shank sometimes welded to it. Traditionally, sterling silver conchos were worn on a belt and used as money or a show of wealth.

cone

a metallic finding used to cap strung beads in necklaces or earrings.

corn stitch

a beading technique also called square or round stitch. It is woven flat and then seamed to make the corn earrings shown in Chapter 11.

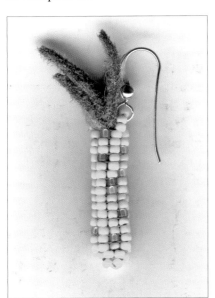

coral

a semiprecious gemstone found in the ocean, usually seen in red, pink, white or black. It is actually a petrified sea creature. Coral is regarded as a status symbol and is almost as popular as turquoise in the pawn industry.

cotton cord

a sturdy cord used for stringing beads and for straps. It is often dyed and waxed.

crimper bead

a special type of bead made of pliable metal which can be used to secure stringing wire when crushed with pliers.

crimper tool

a special tool for flattening and shaping crimper beads.

crow beads

large-holed glass beads often seen on leather fringe.

Delica

a type of Japanese manufactured glass bead known for its laser-cut precision sizing and uniformity of shape. They are also known as cylinder beads.

dentallium shell

a dainty seashell that has a natural cavity for stringing.

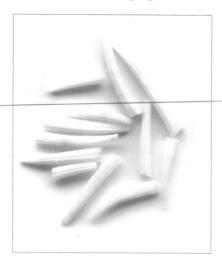

donut

a bead shape usually made from a gemstone to be used as a jewelry component.

dowel

a piece of wooden rod that can be cut to the desired length; used for beading around. A

dowel was used for the key ring project in Chapter 12. Dowels can also be used for beading gourd handles and rattles.

ear wire

a jewelry finding or component for beaded earrings. The one in the photo is called a French wire, but numerous styles, including posts, fish hooks, clip-ons, hoops, lever-backs, and custom designs, such as ear cuffs, are also considered ear wires.

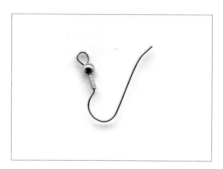

eye pin

a finding used to attach jewelry components.

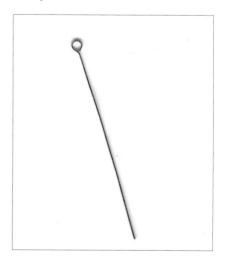

eye screw

a finding or hardware that is threaded for screwing into wood or gourds

fetish

an animal figure that is usually made of gemstone, silver, wood, clay, or shell. Some people attach significance to a characteristic animal trait with which they want to associate themselves or aspire to. For example, a mouse is a small and a seemingly rather insignificant creature with limited vision but remains down-to-earth and observes closely things larger creatures might overlook.

Likewise, an eagle flies high in the sky, has sharp eyesight, and enjoys a lofty aerial view.

findings

hardware typically required to finish jewelry, like ear wires, clasps, pin backs, etc.

fire-polish beads

faceted glass beads manufactured in the Czech Republic. They come in a large variety of colors and finishes. They are fired or heated to a very high temperature to smooth over the sharp facets, giving them a smooth but highly reflective surface. (These are usually called fire-polish beads rather than fire-polished beads.)

flat headpins

a metal pin with a flat base that is used in making earrings and jewelry.

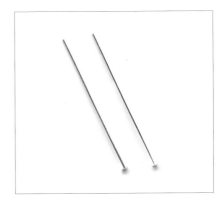

flat-nose pliers

a tool often used in jewelry making that has a smooth, flat jaw surface or a serrated, flat jaw surface. This tool is used for bending relatively soft wire.

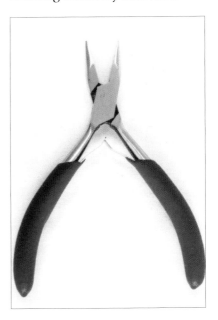

flat peyote stitch

a two-dimensional beading technique that can be seamed to cover a three-dimensional object. It is often used for making bracelets and necklace straps.

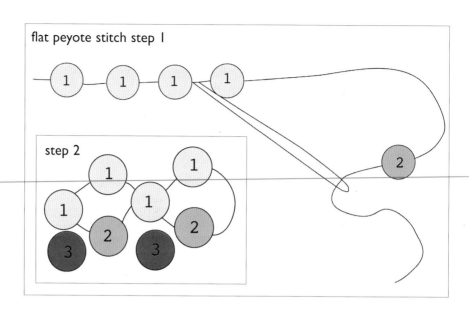

flat peyote stitch step 1

step 2

---

flat round peyote stitch

a beading technique used to make three-dimensional baskets.

fretting

a beading technique used to sew a beaded edge onto leather or fabric.

fringe

strands of leather or beads used to hang from a beaded object or

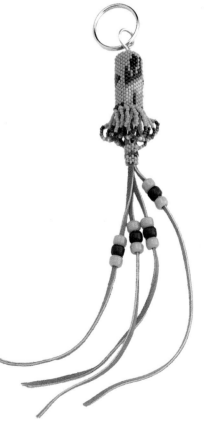

gem chips

small pieces of gemstones that are polished and drilled for use as beads.

gourd

a fruit related to the pumpkin and squash that is dried and used to make rattles, bowls, ladles, birdhouses, or other ornaments.

gourd stitch

a beading technique used to cover a three-dimensional object, also called peyote stitch or one of its many variations.

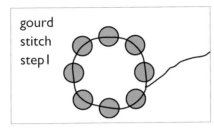

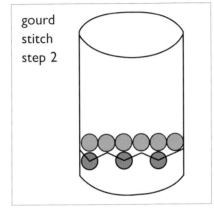

half-hitch knot

also called an in-line knot, the needle is passed under the thread and through the loop.

hook clasp

a common jewelry-closure finding; also called a hook and eye.

horizontal netting

a beading technique done on the horizontal plane and that is very useful for covering oddly shaped three-dimensional objects. See Chapter 16.

Huichol lace

a netting stitch, named after an American Indian tribe in northern Mexico, which is also called horizontal, round, circular, or flat netting.

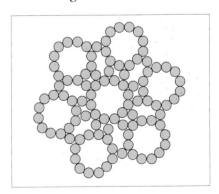

inside-color beads
transparent colored or clear beads with a different color inside.

iris beads
beads with an iridescent finish.

jewelry cement
a sturdy adhesive for gluing glass, metal, and gemstones.

key ring
a finding used for holding keys.

leather lace
long strips of thin leather used to make fringe, straps, and more.

lobster-claw clasp
a metal finding for attaching bracelets or necklaces.

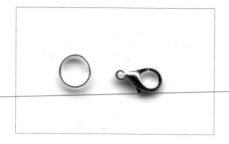

loom stitch
also called square stitch. See Loom or Square-Stitch Graph on p. 110.

luminous beads
beads with neon or astro-brite colors inside the bead.

luster beads
manufacturers' name for opaque beads with a pearllike finish.

matte-finish beads
beads with a frosted, velvety nonshiny texture on the outside

metal earring hoop
a metal hoop with a ring attached for adding an ear wire or charm.

metallic beads
beads with a thin shiny metal surface finish. Because the finish has a tendency to rub off, an acrylic fixative is recommended.

metallic thread
a specialty thread made from metal filament that comes in a variety of colors.

nail polish
a clear acrylic liquid useful in beadwork for sealing knots on beading thread because of its delicate applicator brush.

needle-nose pliers
a tool used for bending rings on soft wire to attach findings; also called round-nose pliers.

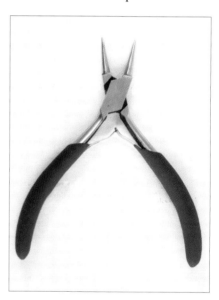

off-loom weaving
a number of stitches generally considered to be bead weaving that do not involve the use of a loom.

opaque beads

solid-colored beads that you cannot see light or thread through.

peak bead

(our invented term) when using the technique of circular netting in Chapters 14 and 16, the term refers to the center bead. For example, if you are adding five beads, the peak bead is the third one, or the one in the middle.

pearl knotting cord

a special type of cord used for stringing and knotting between pearls. It is usually made of a synthetic, like polyester, but it is also made of silk and sold on a card with a needle attached.

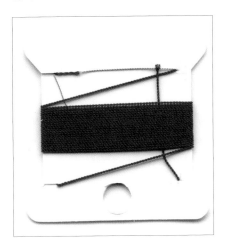

peyote

a cactus plant used in native ceremonies.

peyote stitch

a general term referring to several techniques for covering a three-dimensional object, also referred to as gourd stitch, round peyote, circular peyote, odd-count peyote, even-count peyote, flat peyote, round flat peyote, 2-drop peyote, and 3-drop peyote stitch. Also see the Peyote-Stitch Graph on p. 119.

pin back

a piece of metal hardware that can be attached on the back of beaded jewelry.

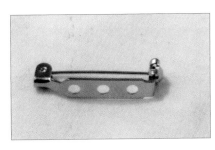

point bead

(our invented term) when using the circular-netting technique for making the three-dimensional basket in Chapter 14, the term applies to a bead used between sections of beads. At the point bead, you can begin increasing the height of the circular netting to help build the walls.

pony beads

glass beads often used for stringing projects.

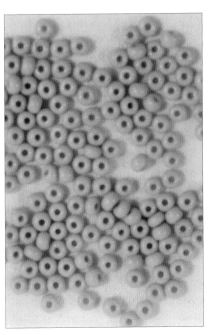

porcupine quills

hairlike structures used as beads.

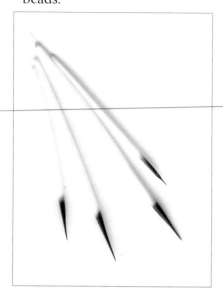

right-angle weave

a beadwork stitch that makes a chain with a foundation of four beads.

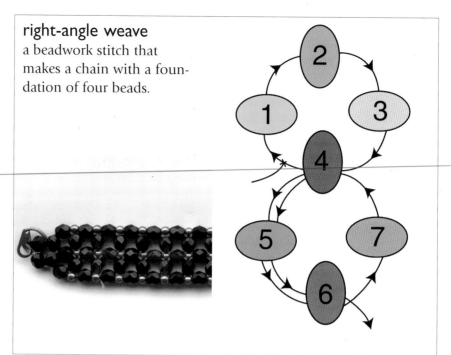

round-nose pliers

a tool used for bending rings on soft wire to attach findings; also called needle-nose pliers. (See photo under needle-nose pliers.)

round stitch

a beading technique; also called square stitch and corn stitch.

seed beads

small glass beads that come in tubes or are strung into hanks.

silver-lined beads

colored beads with a sparkly silver lining. These beads tend to have square holes which reflect light.

seed beads

Sonora

a desert region in the Southwest United States and northwestern Mexico.

Sonora weave

a vertical netting technique. See Chapter 2 for details.

spacer bars

bone, horn, hair, leather, or metal bars drilled with holes for stringing beads.

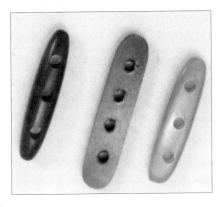

split ring

a jewelry component to attach a clasp to a bracelet or necklace.

square stitch

a beading technique; also called corn stitch and round stitch. See Chapter 11. Also see the Loom or Square-Stitch Graph on p. 110-`.

stop bead

a bead tied onto the end of beading thread to keep the beads from falling off.

stringing wire

nylon coated wire cable to string beads available in a variety of gauges

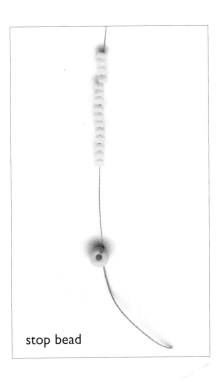

stop bead

thread bridge

the small piece of thread between beads visible at the top of a row of beads, used to connect and anchor them. The Apache weave, or brick stitch, uses a thread bridge in the base row to anchor the beads for attaching the next row of beads.

tie tack

a metal finding to pin a beaded object onto clothing like a tie, collar, or lapel.

transparent beads

clear or colored beads that transmit light which allows you to see through them.

vertical netting

a stitch woven on the vertical plane, also called Sonora weave. See Chapter 2 for details.

visual aids

magnifier glasses and beading lamps with magnification lenses used to help people see better while working with small beads.

white glue

water-based adhesive that is nontoxic and dries clear.

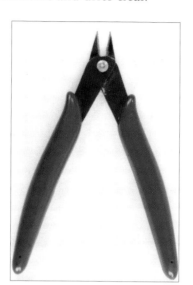

wire cutters

a tool designed to cut metal like stringing wire, eye pins, and light-gauge silver.

wooden beads

small pieces of wood, shaped into beads and with a hole bored into the center. Machine-made or hand-carved wooden beads are on the market. Here's a sample of hand-carved wooden beads made by the Yoeme tribe in Arizona.

INDEX

ACKNOWLEDGMENTS

I would like to express my thanks to the many beadwork designers who generously shared their techniques and enthusiasm and contributed to this book—Gale Manning, Jonathan Pulley, Judy Gorman, Laura Moreno, Shelia Vinson, and Terri La Brosse. A special thanks to Linda and Jack Pennington, owners of Jay's of Tucson whose family of traders has supplied generations of artists with materials they need for their creative work. I am also grateful to the grandmothers of the San Carlos Apache tribe, who have graciously shared their beadwork knowledge with me and to the many beadwork teachers who keep the traditional art of beadwork alive.

I am deeply grateful to my late mother, Anna Flores, for introducing me to beads and teaching me to create many beautiful things. My mother, a most honorable woman, showed me how to walk in beauty.

I would also like to thank my husband, Robert Geary, who is the computer genius behind the scenes, and my grown children, Jonny Pulley and Anna Pulley, who have provided me with invaluable technical assistance. In addition, I must acknowledge Dana Muller, who inspired me to write this book, and Jeanette Green, my editor, who made it possible.

ABOUT THE AUTHOR

Theresa Flores Geary, Ph.D., taught by her mother and elders from the San Carlos Apache tribe, has been creating beadwork since age 14. She has retired from an active career as a clinical psychologist and served, most recently, as a family psychologist for the Pascua Yaqui tribe in Tucson, Arizona.

Besides making jewelry and other beaded objects, she has developed a line of self-instructional bead kits called Native Beads that she sells to museums, gift shops, and retail stores. The kits are also used in after-school programs, summer recreation programs, rehabilitation and drug treatment centers, cultural activities, and specialized therapy programs for the youth and elderly.

Dr. Geary has been a pioneer in the use of bead therapy used to help heal both physical and psychological conditions as well as everyday stress. Many institutions with inpatient care such as psychiatric hospitals, drug and alcohol treatment centers, prisons, and nursing homes, have also seen the benefits of bead therapy. Cultural programs and rehabilitation after-care programs have also championed bead therapy.

She currently teaches beadwork classes at Jay's of Tucson, a retail/wholesale business that specializes in American Indian arts.

She lives in Tucson, Arizona, with her husband, son, and daughter. She has two more sons who live in Florida with their families.